THE BLUE MUSEUM

Sisyphus Press
P. O. Box 330098
San Francisco CA 94133
Cous@philcousineau.net

First Printing: September 2004
Second Printing: January 2005
Third Printing : April 2005
Fourth Printing: September 2005
Fifth Printing: June 2006
Sixth Printing: June 2008

Library of Congress Catalog Card Number:
Printed in the United States of America
Design by Richard Seibert

Grateful acknowledgment to the following publishers, where the
following poems first appeared:

J. P. Tarcher Publishers, Inc., for "For My Father Who Never
     Made It to Paris"
Harper San Francisco, for "Sleeping Beauties"
The Scream, for "Music in the Wood" and "Memoricide"
Big Scream, for "Pimp Painters" and "Sanding"
Journey magazine, for "Lightning in St. Chapelle"
Synapse Magazine, for "Proteus"
Jung Society News, for "The Genius" and "Vincent"

Cover Photograph: The White Chapel in a Blue World, Mykonos, Greece, 1993

BOOKS BY THE AUTHOR

To *Mort Rosenblum* and *Jeannette Hermann*
friends and patrons of the Blue Museum

THE
BLUE
MUSEUM

Poems by *PHIL COUSINEAU*

SISYPHUS PRESS

EXHIBITIONS

I

The imagination is a deep-sea diver
that rakes the bottom of the poet's mind
and dredges up sleeping images. . .
If we go deep enough, we may discover
the secret place where our key images
have been stored since childhood.
———— *Stanley Kunitz*

SPHINX

Tides of silence wash over the marble bones
of the ancient quarters of Alexandria,
submerged in the murky harbor.

How do you make mute stones speak?

Consider the skin-diver hovering in the turbid depths,
a few murky feet away from a long lost stone sphinx.
He's holding a waterproof sketchpad in his hands.
A question is carving doubt in his mind.
He's floating like an astronaut in the blue-blackening depths of space,
poised like a painter before a mockingly empty canvas,
as spellbound as Oedipus before his own stone-faced inquisitor
on the dusky road outside doomed Thebes.

What is it you need to know?

It's impossible to see what the diver is writing down
in the glossy travel magazine photograph, but still
I lean into it, trying to imagine his watery words.
The riddle he's asked to solve is unfathomable —

What is the oldest word known to man?

But I've got to have a crack at it,
even if it keeps me awake for centuries.
I need to hear how he answers the women-breasted,
lion-pawed, eagle-winged sphinx, who asks him,

"I've got to know why you keep writing when
   you're underwater, just this far from drowning?"

The diver stares down the impertinent sphinx
as he hovers above the sea floor.
Her hollowed-out eyes follow him.
She's stymied, thinking,
"He can't answer my riddle,
   he knows I'll devour him, yet
   he keeps on taking those damned notes."

   What is the sound of one hand writing?

The diver rolls his eyes,
takes a deep breath,
answers wordlessly:

   Silence.

Then murmurs through
his steaming mask,
"Now go jump off a cliff."

AFTER A PHRASE ABANDONED BY NERUDA

Winter comes on strong,
like words full of deep vowels.
I wake up dreaming of summer wind
playing in the dark hair of the one I love.
We are dancing in a torch-lit taverna
on an island floating somewhere
between Piraeus and paradise.
Olive-scented air is there,
bouzouki music thrums everywhere.

Our lives spin on the axis of such dreams.
They turn on hinges of change as swift
and unsettling as the white-horsed waves
coming and going on the storm-tossed sea.
And with these torqued-up dreams comes the vision
that "the coming years will be a lovely blue,"
the poet's promise of a deeper hue,
the lover's plea for the end of solitude.

I had no one to tell this to but you
who knew the angry shade of
bruised boxer blue that scarred
my soul long before we were
dreamed by the dream
dreaming you,
dreaming me.

THE MUSIC IN THE WOOD

The smoky-eyed man in the old Dublin music shop
leans over the oak counter and squints at the
guitars, flutes, pennywhistles, drums, and fiddles
that hang on the paneled wall like notes on wrinkled sheet music.
He adjusts his woolen cap, then lifts his whiskered chin,
in the old Irish way, towards a goatskin drum.
The rumpled shop owner takes it down, caressing it as he
hands it over, saying by way of conversation,
"A brilliant instrument, lad. Did you know what yer man says
about these drums, that there's nothing like the sound
of a *bodhran* to rise the blood in a man?"
"Aye, you're dead right," says he, thrumming
his nicotine-stained fingers over the taut skin.
He sees a dust-covered fiddle in a dark corner.
"Oh, you're eyeing the gypsy piece.
Finely burnished instrument, it 'tis."
He lowers his voice, "Did ye know what they say,
that they'll hold old melodies in the wood forever?
Aye, and that a discerning, God-fearing
ear can still hear them."
The visitor furrows his brow, mutters,
"You don't say, you don't say."
He trades the drum for the fiddle,
plucks a single string, pulls it close to his ear,
as if listening for faraway music.
"Oh, it's grand, it's grand," says he.
"It sounds golden, like honey from the hive.
It's *alive*, it's *alive*."

On the other side of the world,
a man salvages long-drowned logs
from the peat-darkened depths of Lake Superior,
then dries, cuts and sells the iridescent wood
to violin makers for what he calls their "acoustic resonance,"
oscillating evidence of the hidden music of the world,
the saving grace of slumbering chords.
He believes in the dormant power of lost melodies
recovered from the discordant world. He trusts in
the rustling sounds wrenched from stubborn silence.
He knows there is an undertone, the murmur
that strengthens the soul, the music
within all things that lasts
for reasons reason cannot hear,
much less fathom.

I remember being beguiled by a single blue note long ago.
It slowly rose from the silty bottom of the world,
then broke through the rippling surface of my life
like a sudden rapture.

If I listen with my third ear,
I will hear it again. We don't
know ourselves until
we turn into music.

FOOTPRINTS

He thought he was alone.
We all do.

He believed God had abandoned him.
Don't we all?

For years the pain of being shipwrecked hurt like blue blazes.
It always does.

Then Crusoe saw the footprints
In the hot sand.

He never made a conscious decision to follow.
He just ran for his life,

For sudden joys, like griefs,
Confound at first.

His feet fitting perfectly inside
The cool footprints

Left behind by the stranger,
The helpmeet, the unmet,

Longed for
Friend.

THE TASTE OF BLUE

I love the way the world
tastes blue whenever I savor it,
as it does now as I drop green
dollar bills into the pulsating neon

jukebox, and swoon to the soaring
voice of Gianni Schucchi singing
Puccini's "O Mio Babbino Caro,"
and revel in the way she transports me

to the forested hills above Genoa
where I once furtively watched
a madonna of a mother singing
tenderly to her sad-eyed baby

on a park bench
with no one but God
listening to the way she transformed
her doubled heartbeat into prayerful music

that lifted her child's spirits
on wings of love,
all this of a summer's day,
a blue heaven of a summer's day.

WINDOWS AND DOORS
for Jo

I dreamt of you standing before a window by the sea,
in a place that sounded something like Brittany.
You were gazing with your thousand-yard stare
at ten thousand-year-old bluestone megaliths,
which were poised along the shore, ancient sentinels,
strong and steady, as you make me feel
when we walk together, hands entwined,
with the growing strength of oaks
sending out life-seeking roots
through solid rock.

And then you murmured,
I knew I would be the one.

Those dreamquake words rumbled in me
as if another late-night California tremor
had shaken our house on the hill.
When my eyes opened our world
was not shattered, but still standing,
with you by the window in a wispy white dress,
sunlight blithely dancing on your bare shoulders
and spangling your long black hair.
My eyes kissed your windblown soul.
You turned to me and playfully asked
where I'd been, as if you didn't know
about the small hidden door
in our house of dreams.

YOKO'S YES

You walk in.
There's a white stepladder you're supposed to climb.
Near the ceiling there's a note hanging from a string
and a magnifying glass suspended from the frame.
You use it to look at the tiny inscription.
It's written in India ink and says "Yes."

I see this guy as he comes down the ladder.
He doesn't seem excited. He's in a blue funk. He looks at me,
shrugs, smiles thinly, stays a little while, and leaves.

*It's a great relief when you get up the ladder and you look
through the spyglass and it doesn't say No! or Fuck you!*

I had a couple students helping me with the display,
One of them said, "I think that's ... *John Lennon* ... of the Beatles."
He said it very slowly, so it sounded interesting. It was funny.

*It says YES . . . No negative, smash-the-piano-with-a-
hammer, break-the-sculpture boring, negative crap.
That YES made me stay.*

Two weeks later we met at another art show in the Village.
Hmm, I thought, so I've met a guy who plays the same game I play.
The rest, as they say in these things, is history.

CATCH AS CATCH CANNES, 1986

Dry twig brooms scratch rain-burnished cobblestones.
Corrugated metal gates rattle and windows yawn open
in the blue-tiled café on the town square.
Melting ice gurgles in fish market gutters.
The song of the town bakery's oven sings
with the melody of fresh *croissant amandes*.

Dawn in southern France.
Every morning a fresh beginning.
The rebirth of light so golden and delicious you can spread it over
your five-franc pastries, so dextrous it crawls across the sandstone
wall like fast-growing grapevines, so tremulous it shimmers
with every toll of cathedral bells. A soul-soothing light
for jaded film critics and faded movie fans,
who've been plunged into darkness for eleven days
in search of some mad form of endarkenment,
their fair share of shadowplay salvation,
the quickening of light's lingering mystery,
maybe a flicker of entertainment,
in no particular order.

Pure sweet light streaming like warm caramel
over the seaside town's time-smoothed stones,
redeeming the dream of electric shadows
to resolve the unnamable plots that underscore our lives.
Sneak previews, snarky reviews, surreptitious glances
of the famous Italian actresses's plunging décolleté,
or the tantrum turned by the smarmy English actor
dying to be back in the limelight.

It's an ancient dream that light creates the world.
It's a perennial hope that light will come again and redeem us,
the old Platonic ideal that declaims glorious truth
is just outside the lip of the dark cave, the
next new thing that reclaims the magic lantern
as the means for transformation of chimeras into reality,
age-old lustrous longings, all,
for moving images that might light
our way to paradise.

A bold belief that flickers of light will entrance,
enchant and electrify us, a shadow-strewn memory
of ritualized catharsis that will purge us,
a hope against hope that messages
from the spirit world
just might save us.

Or at least explain
us to ourselves,
in a matinee
kind of way,
for, oh, ninety
minutes
or so.

WITH JACK, AGE FOUR, IN THE CAR

We drove in darkness,
the amber lights of Sonoma
receding in my rearview mirror,
shadows leaping like thieves
from eucalyptus trees
along the night road.

How do you lead a child
into the darkness and out again?

What can you say to your young son
after he watches you watching soldiers
shoot children on the evening news?
What can you say when he turns your bones blue
by asking you from the backseat of the car,
"Please, Papa, hold my hand.
It's dark all round me."

The dark word had never sounded so ominous.
I reach across the back seat, feeling velveteen
darkness on my fingertips, and clasp his
trembling hand in my best tough — and —
tender grasp, then hear him whisper,
as if to reassure *me*:
"Just until it gets light again, Papa."
And now driving one-handed, I listen
for the reassuring sound of sleep, remember
the moment I held him for the first time,
all crinkled and crying, blinking and trying

to open his gummed-up eyes,
startled by all that light
after all that darkness.

Hurtling home past long-abandoned railroad tracks
and farm land lost to grapevines, I spin
the green-glowing dial of the car radio
and hear Bruce Springsteen wailing
like a lost locomotive about how
he'd "Drive All Night"
just to be with her,
his love,
his life.

And hearing that lonesome moan, I sing along
until I feel my dead father's voice vibrating
in my throat, sing until I hear traces
of my own voice in my son's as he cries,
"Papa, how much longer? How much longer
is it going to be dark?"

Only then did the words spring free,
the lie I told to tell the longer truth,
"Don't worry, buddy, we'll be home soon.
I won't let the darkness hurt you."

PITCH DARK

One night, late in '48, the Tigers are playing
the Senators at old Griffith Stadium.
The old game is unfolding languorously
in the seventh inning when the Tiger pitcher
goes into his wind-up. He rears back,
kicks high and —
the ballpark lights flicker,
flash, and sputter out,
leaving the field
pitch-dark.
The batter flinches,
the catcher flails, the umpire lurches.
The infielders and outfielders flop to the ground,
covering their capped heads with their raggedy leather mitts.
The fans in the stands listen for the crack of the bat,
hear only the sizzle of surging electricity in the light towers.
Five freeze-framed seconds later —
the towers of light blink back on,
revealing nine ballplayers and the man in blue
lying flat on the field, eyes clinched shut, hiding
from the one play they'd never practiced.
The only player still standing is the wide-eyed
pitcher whose arm is frozen in mid-air,
looking like an old-time baseball card.
He alone knows he never threw
the ball.

SLOW DISSOLVE

My friend tells me with a daughterly hush in her voice
that she can't meet me at Gladstone's down on the beach
because she has to see her mother, even though —
and then her voice goes tremolo —
"Even though the Alzheimer's,
well, kind of *vaporizes* her memory
a few minutes after I leave."

Her triple-carom comment
ricochets inside my head,
then hurls me down a black-hole of memory,
like the coffee cup spiraling away into another
universe in Hawking's *A Brief History of Time*,
like the darkroom enlargers of the Russian photographers
who air-brushed Stalin's enemies out of existence.
Her heartbreaking words trigger
the *slow dissolve* button
on memory's editing table,
cutting from real life to reel life,
telephone to television,
the distant dialing in of a late-night movie.
Of a sudden my soul is roving
eight thousand miles away
to the movie set of Fellini's
phantasmagorical *Roma*,
and I'm stunned to find myself
assistant director to the genius who says,
"I'm no artist; I just film my dreams."
Scrambling with the *sandhogs*,

underground construction workers,
I'm in the cab of a colossal drilling machine
boring a tunnel hundreds of feet below 1960s Rome
when we crash through the scumbled blue stucco walls
of a two-thousand-year-old Roman villa.

Caught in the holdfast grip of reverie
I step across the threshold between two lost worlds
and discover a labyrinth of rooms
haunted with frescoes as fresh
as the day they were painted,
aristocratic Romans undergoing mystery rites,
shopkeepers dining and conversing,
children playing with tops and hoops.
                              Seconds later
there's a sudden *rush* of fresh air
pouring into the time-locked chamber
like damned up water through a hole in a dike.
I watch with horror as the newly liberated light
dances across the preserved frescoes
for the first time in two thousand years,
dissolving their very molecules,
disintegrating the stories
waiting to be told.

Shaking off the reverie as if it had been a seizure,
returning slowly back into my body like one of those
spiraling lost souls in a William Blake feverdream painting,
I manage to say to my heart-reeling friend,
"Don't worry. She knows, she *knows*.
A part of your mom remembers your visits, her *soul*,

that's where you're still connected."
"You *really* think so?" she asks, plaintively.
Her terror of being forgotten is palpable,
reviving my own fear that unflexed memory
is too much like silver nitrate film that's been
hidden in the back of a closet for decades,
gumming up, dissolving — or exploding —
when finally exposed to oxygen.

I should know.
I'm overwhelmed by stroboscopic memories,
flashing black light images of things that may
or may not have ever happened.
I can barely remember my last visit with my father,
but replay it anyway, night after night after night.
I was hungover, not alert enough to know
he was trying to tell me he was dying,
"I don't know how much longer I have left."
Just thirty-two, I didn't believe a guy
could lose his father that young.
I huddled deep into my black leather jacket
that still stank of motorcycle fumes,
felt my heart shrink-wrapped by his cracking voice,
the icy finality with which we shook hands
in the doorway of his apartment.

These words are all that's keeping
the memory from fading away.
They're all I remember
from our last visit.
It ain't enough.

THE TRUE MEANING OF NOSTALGIA

If I hadn't remembered my father dancing every New Year's Eve
as zanily as Zorba on the sun-bleached beach of southern Crete,
trying in vain to keep with the beat of *bouzouki* music
on the soundtrack of *Never on Sunday* that spun lustily
on our old Philco hi-fi console turntable;
if I hadn't recalled the photograph of the marble-muscled statue
of Poseidon he clipped out of *Time* magazine and pasted into my boyhood
scrapbook in between his press releases about Ford's hottest new
test-cars and postcards of Rubens' full-bosomed women;
if I hadn't discovered his *Detroit Free Press's* travel section,
the one devoted to the Greek islands on the coffee-stained
television tray next to the faux-leather easychair he died in;
if I had never dreamt of Odysseus
sailing with the thousand black-hulled ships
across the wine-dark, god-fermented sea
out of a sense of sheer loyalty to his fellow kings,
as well as deep conviction that beauty [read: Helen]
was a virtue worth dying for;
if all this hadn't been pressed
like a seal into the wax of my soul,
then maybe I wouldn't have shivered
with phantom limb recall the first time
I swam in Homer's sea, walked the wind-buffed
walls of Troy, and ran down the beach
like one of the death-frenzied Greek victors
racing in the funeral games to celebrate *life*.
Oh, but I did, I did.

As if memory had shipwrecked
along the shoals of my still grieving heart,
like Odysseus who could not get home
again till he remembered
how much he'd forgotten,
which is really what made him
everyman's *no man*
for the next twenty-eight
centuries.

So I ask you, what is this vagrant thing called *memory*,
this wandering mother of the muses, those serenaders
of the gods, inspirer of the arts and the first *museum?*
What is the bittersweet force she brings,
the blue angels of remembering,
the blue demons of forgetting,
the pressing down on our hearts
by this homesickness, this centrifugal pull
calling us back to where it all began,
asking us to remember what will claw at our hearts
if it disappears, taunting us to tell about it
in our own *nostoi*, our own *going home* stories
that try to capture the inevitable sadness
of life's passing, this tantalizing that asks,
What now,
voyager?

THE HOUSE OF MEMORY

Every human being comes to earth,
Wrote Kierkegaard, *with sealed orders.*

What are yours?

Have you unsealed your orders
As the houses of memory are burning?

Thenadays, during classical times and again the Renaissance,
Poets, orators, politicians, philosophers practiced the art
Of memory, devised elaborate systems of recall,
Such as conjuring up an image of a villa, a theater,
A stadium, or a palace, and in each room, row, or section,
Or corridor they would place something they needed to remember:
A word, a phrase, a series of numbers,
So memory could be stamped onto the soul
Like a signet ring impressed on hot wax.

A great and beautiful invention is memory . . .
If you pay attention and direct your mind.
What you hear, place on what you know.

When time came to recall the memory in a speech,
a debate, an argument, or storytelling session,
the honey-tongued speaker walked for miles
through the corridors of the house of memory,
retrieving the needed words and images
from his own many-roomed mind.

Recollection is the recovery of knowledge
Or sensation which one had before . . .
To remember was to put everything in its proper place.

Where are the memory houses now
When we need them, now when our collective memory
Is being *de*constructed rather than constructed,
Now when the past is disdained because
It takes up too much room in our memory chips?
Where are the mnemonic marvels that will help us
Rub memory till it glisters, recalling the towns we were born in,
The white-washed steeples we prayed under,
The maple trees we carved our lovers names into?
If we don't need to learn hundreds of plays by heart
Like the actors at Shakespeare's Globe Theater,
How do we handle the banishing of memory?

Your orders are to forget everything
You've heard that told you not to remember.
You might think of something worth living for.

And we wonder why we dream so mightily,
So lucidly, about the house we grew up in,
The marks we left on the cave walls,
The sparks we knocked off the flint.

WRITING IN THE DARK

When he realized there was no hope for rescue
The Russian lieutenant groped his way through
The luciferous dark to his corner desk
Deep in the steel-ribbed bowels of the submarine.
The bones of his hands ached as he removed
Paper and pen from the sliding metal drawer,
And he conjured up the way the summer light
Of St. Petersburg played in his fiancée's long blonde hair,
How her breath blew softly on his cheek, and how
Her rosebud lips slipped across his mouth like a promise.
The iron walls creaked; seawater leaked in.
The officer steadied his stinging fingers.
He slowed down his breathing
So the last of the oxygen would
Last a few minutes longer.
Then he began his last letter
With the simple truth:
"I am writing blindly."
He wrote as the darkness thickened
Around the blue flare of his last matches.
He wrote as his lungs ached from the rising pressure,
And his ears bled from the noise of rivets popping from the walls,
And the engines, dynamos, and pumps rumbling,
Then falling silent.
He wrote until he could breathe no more.
Weeks later, the letter was found
Under his luridly bloated hand
By a rescue team who delivered it to his fiancée,
As if from another world.
It's later than you think.

MEMORICIDE

Black snow fell over Sarajevo,
darkening the midday sky with ashes
from the million and a half books burning
in what was once the national library.
The old librarian raced through shell-pocked streets,
his face reddening from the torrid heat pouring
out of the knot of smoking ruins where
he had spent a lifetime rescuing words
from oblivion. Defying the withering fire of the snipers,
he stood on the steps of the smoldering building
wanting to save — something, anything — even
the single sheet of cindered paper that drifted towards him
through the singed air, still holding fire from the inferno.
Catching the paper, which glowed in his hand
like a black and white negative held up
to the red light inside a photographer's darkroom,
he glared at what was once a page from a holy book,
an illuminated manuscript, and couldn't smell the skin
of his fingertips burning as he tried reading from what seemed
to be the last page of the last book on earth.
With time on fire, history incinerated,
the brittle page flaked and flared, then
vanished, leaving blue and gold and red ash
on his cold, numb hands.
Staring into the fiery ruins, he wondered
when he could start rebuilding.

THE GARDEN

In love we learn to touch and let go,
knowing the moments when to dig
the mood indigo.

When people spark that conflagration of clarity
between them they touch each other
as tenderly as those old barbers
who trained with straight-razors on
lightly lathered balloons.

I want to interlace arms and legs
and make love with you in a turquoise-tiled
room lit by tortoises who roam around our bed
with candles on their shells, like those in
the harems of Constantinople palaces.

I need to find a paradise of words
to describe how I found my second heart,
when I found you, as alive as birdsong
and lovely as lavender in the rolling
hills above the garden
wet with rain.

Ampus, Provence,
1993

THE STILLNESS OF THE WORLD AFTER GREECE
after Lars Gustafsson

There must have been a world before classical
Greece, a world before the long echoes of Sophocles
in the amphitheater of Epidaurus, a world before
the serene dignity in the speeches of Pericles,
a world before the quiet miracle of the sculpture
of the *Delphi Charioteer*, but what kind of a world?
A world of unrest, fury and discord,
and everywhere the clangor of clashing
ideas, where the memory of Hector's calm embrace
of his trembling son on the fateful walls of Troy,
the tranquil happiness of Epictetus,
the lucid madness in the rituals at Eleusis had not
yet initiated anyone into the mysteries of death and rebirth,
never touched the soul.
Isolated lands
where the calm is shattered by old warriors' axes,
the rasping of ships' keels hauled ashore,
and, like a song, chisels singing in the depths of marble;
porpoises friskily playing in the pearly sea,
the smell of salty sea in a child's nostrils,
and nowhere Heraclitus, Phidias, or Socrates,
nowhere the philosopher's silent roar of freedom,
the painter's balm of beauty, the world in a frenzy
before the blue and white stillness in the soul of Greece.

II

I must keep quiet for a little space
and then walk very slowly along
that bright sound of pain
towards the blue, blue wave.
What bliss there is in blueness.
I never knew how blue blueness could be.
—— *Vladimir Nabokov*

THE BLUE MUSEUM

The fisherman of Mithyrum, having cast their their nets into the sea, drew
them in and discovered a head carved from the wood of an olive tree...

—— *Pausanius, second century*

I.

There on the briny shores of Naxos,
on the edge of the ultramarine sea,
where the scorchingly hot sun
blisters old stones,
makes bold light sing,
I sit on a gently swaying wooden pier
watching an aged fisherman
with salt-swollen hands empty
gleaming nets of flailing fish.
Calmly, he catches them in midair as they
try to defy gravity and evade fate,
the single blow from the old wooden
mallet of his softly singing, black-shawled wife.
There where the island sky hurries into heavenly blue
and the whitewashed windmills creak and groan,
the fisherman lays the fish down on the pier
like communion hosts on an altar,
mumbling to each of them in
the dark-keeled words of his ancestors.

2.

His name is Manoles and his face
is crimped with wrinkles, hard-earned life-lines
revealing the map of his secret knowledge
of the cobalt blue world that engulfs him.

He smiles like a pelican with a good haul in his beak,
squats down on the pier with a fistful of dripping net.
Methodically, he begins to mend the severed threads
while naming the fish he caught out at sea,
nouns that sounds to me as exotic and remote
as Homer's supply list for the thousand ships bound for Troy.
Without looking up from his task, Manoles says
that on certain mornings, with the mist
"as gray as the eyes of goddess Athena,"
he sometimes finds strange things tangled in his nets,
"Old coins. Old urns. Old statues."
His voice drops weightlessly,
then seems to float on the salty air
like the corks he fastens to his nets.
"The sea, she is full of treasure from ships that — "
and frustrated by his fractured English,
he shapes his rope-burned hands into a ship
whose prow dips in and out of the glittering
waves and, smiling like an old sea lion, adds,
"That is why we call her
the blue museum."

3.

I gaze out over the neptune-blue waters,
listening intently to the lullaby
sung by the wave-washed shore,
trying to fathom the world of submerged galleries
filled with mysterious riches found in neolithic dugout canoes,
the lost treasure of storm-sunk cargo boats,
the abandoned loot of overloaded galleons,
submerged triremes that once cleaved the sea,
argosies that never reached home, long-

40

lost vessels in a swirling blur of
turquoise-tinged sea water

gasp! imagine it y—

that tumbled marble gods and bronze warriors,
tumbled coins, cannons, warrior's bows, iron swords,
tumbled copper ingots, glass bottles, victors vases,   *falling*
tumbled jars of Greek olive oil, Irish gold, Baltic amber, African ebony,
tumbled cylinder seals from Assyria and mosaics from Babylon,
tumbled lead anchors, iron cauldrons and silver candelabras,
tumbled mammoth bones, hippopotamus tusks, ostrich eggshells,
tumbled gold bullion, silver religious icons, silks and damasks,
and tumbled an orgy's worth of amphoras of wine,
which may be why the sea is so wine-dark,
afterall.

Five fathoms deep the treasure fell,
centuries deep they fell, as good as gone forever,
down through history's merciless black water whirlpool,
until rediscovered now and again,
here and there, in the back of beyond,
as chance discoveries in Greek trawling nets,   *greece*
on the dropped anchors of Italian boats,   *Turkey*
in the groping hands of Turkish sponge divers,   *Italy*
all of whom looked but did not see
beauty, value, worth, purpose or meaning
in corroded figures or contorted icons
they couldn't understand, which is why
treasures were tossed back into the foaming sea   *you got me there*
or dropped into sizzling lime kilns back on land
to be born again as gleaming whitewash
for the island's cottages.

4.

"Manoles, what do you do with the statues?
Do you take them home with you,
do you sell them to tourists?"
The cold clear island light silhouettes his face
as he knits his forehead and ponders his response
like an old philosopher musing over a challenge
in the nearby agora two hundred centuries ago.
He watches his wife fasten the fish onto a line of rope
from the mast of their boat to a gnarled olive tree
whose leaves glisten like quicksilver in the cobbled square.
When she's finished he beckons her over
and slips a sprig of fuchsia into her graying hair.
"Oh, I give them back to the authorities,"
he says to me, shrugging like a sail in the wind.
"They are like fish that are too small
and must go back into the sea.
I could sell them, but then I couldn't sleep.
My father, he told me they were made
by our father's father's fathers for us
to look at so we might remember
things we are not supposed to forget."
I'm dying to ask him, "Remember *what?*"
but he's already looking away, assuming
I know which things are forgotten at our peril,
and gazing affectionately out to sea,
as if recognizing old friends or adventures
in the shapes of the white-capped waves.
Smiling, he sniffs the tangy air of the sea,
pours a few glistening drops of olive oil
into the sea lapping at his feet,

a ritual offering to Poseidon to ask
for calm waters when he sets sail
after midnight.

5.

This is the moment
I've been waiting for
for two long years
while circling the world,
the moment of salvaging
something from my soul-capsizing
years in the steel factory back home,
the storm-drenched violence,
the ancient blood feuds,
that will not let me sleep.
The cool blue evening is coming on,
announced by the clanging of taverna owners' tambourines,
the clanking of gangways from docking ferries,
the cawing of seagulls, the moon-wooed song of the sea,
the cooing of young lovers on the piers.
I am all of twenty-two,
alone on this moon-washed pier,
half a world away from the stench of phosphate,
the relentless pounding of steel presses,
the savagery of the war that gouged holes
in the hearts of my hometown friends.
A year down the road and I'm still feeling my ribs
being wedged open by some steel-fingered
force I cannot put a name on,
a god, a song, a word, a second
heart trying to enter my chest.

just when my ribs were starting to heal!

Then, one evening,
I read in a dog-earred copy of Epictetus,
"If a man is not happy, it is his own fault."
And the world around me sparkles
with sapphire blue light, a hint
of how ancient ruins
are rebuilt, stone
by stone, story
by story.

    6.
The old fisherman packs his gear.
We promise to meet at Pindar's Taverna
nestled into the sands by the old ruins,
at the earliest midnight on earth,
Mediterranean midnight when
the beveled edge between dusk and dawn,
retsina, *kalamari* and *bouzouki* music,
are most bracing.
Later that night,
I'm luxuriating in the sound of surf,
and reveling in the sight of old couples
with wind-chapped faces and calloused hands
dancing on ancient flagstones,
and plunge into a sea of reverie,
seeking a lost masterpiece
on the sea floor of my soul,
a pensive Athena,
a trident-wielding Poseidon,
a splendid runner from Olympia,
a leering Satyr from Paros,

restless gifts from the sunken
nomads of the deep.

Wonder washes over me like spindrift,
blessing me with a glimmer of the sweet life,
a glimpse of the ships setting sail
for the forgotten isles of happiness,
reminding me that although the gods may
be grinding the world to dust,
every journey to them brings them back to life,
as slowly happens to me on these god-trodden shores,
over the meandering course of weeks and months
wandering the galleries of the blue museum,
raising my half-submerged soul,
quickening it
for the life
to come.

blurry and blue

III

If indigo was used to draw a fine blue rainbow,
it was taken from the brow of your eyes.
—— *Hafiz*

THE MEANING OF HAPPINESS
after Brendan Behan

The gleam of blueberries
wet with rain
on glacier rock

The swift flow of salmon
in brisk rivers
loud with moonlight

The murmur of lovers,
calling the restless one
in her teeming belly

STARFISH

for Michelle

I run my forefinger
In a spiral pattern
Over her tiny pink hand,

Clinching my eyes to better
Focus on her gentle trust,
Her supple faith,

Which triggers a lovely
Flex of one bold finger
Into an exclamation point,

Then relaxes in recognition
That she has always known me,
That I am her uncle, her family.

For a held-breath moment
Her splayed out hand
Is a starfish

Left gleaming in sunlight
After the sea has receded
In a swarming tide pool,

Its baby-blue veins
Pulsing with new life,
Old rhythms.

Her tiny hand is an omen,
A reflection of submerged forces
Flung from a world beyond,

Deeper than this one,
A glint of beauty left for drifters
To gaze upon with trembling wonder,

To touch, to hold in their hands
So they might feel the sigh
Of eternity slowly grip them,

And hold them fast,
So they are not
Afraid.

Wayne, Michigan
1981

KITES

for Jo

Driving along the Marina Green
on a gloriously clear Sunday afternoon,
the sight of soaring, swooping kites
brings a whirling smile to your lovely face,
moving you to muse, rather wistfully,
"I wonder what birds think of kites?"

I swerve into the parking lot along the bay
thinking about the stray thoughts of seagulls
who just might care about the antic souls
of biplane kites, dragon kites, caterpillar
and great-winged butterfly kites,
who might be as fascinated
as we are by the *whoosh* and *swoosh*
of their ecstatic rising and falling
in slipstreaming winds,
blue streaking thermals.

We take off our shoes to feel the moist green grass
on our toes, then tumble to the ground
to marvel at the zigzagging,
whirligigging, carouseling kites
high in the powder blue sky.
"Don't they have a world of their own?" you ask,
"They must, they've got to have a world of their own,
don't you think? Why should we be the only ones?"
Following your lead, I look up into the sky,
which now seems to invert, flip upside down,

so it feels like I'm peering down through a periscope
into a blue-green sea brimming with schools of phosphorescent fish,
who are presumably learning about the joys of swimming through the air.
"Maybe, just maybe," I say, "birds think of kites
the way that fish think of skin divers,
or bats judge cave explorers —
as crazy intruders into
their private worlds."

Your smile smacks of amusement
at the topsy-turvy thought
of upside down worlds.
With your nudge, the menagerie of kites
with their technicolor streamers transform into sting rays,
squirming yellow eels, whose strings are nowhere to be seen,
souls in flight with minds of their own,
until we trace the kite strings back
to the invisible hands behind
every visible movement.

"Maybe, baby," I say playfully,
"maybe birds wonder if people are the souls of kites,
the source of the thin string of connection,
the breath that gives them life?"

Your gaze follows the flight of birds
darting in between the kites, then
down to the cavorting of two terriers
chasing the kites, inspiring you to say,
with a smile like summer lightning
that makes my heart lurch like a kite

lifted by a sudden surge
of warm wind swarming
in off the bay,

"Animals are the only thing
that make me human."

San Francisco, California
1990

GO-KART

Most people say they don't remember
the first time, and I don't mean sex,
drugs, or rock and roll.

I do.

It's a soft summer morning,
Michigan, circa 1961.
I'm eight, maybe nine years old.
No one's home, no friends around.
I've got a case of the sweet abandons.

My bare feet are glad to feel the warmth of the sun
on the driveway as I lean over the I-shaped wooden go-kart
I've made with my best buddy, Mark, my hands are happy
adjusting the steering ropes, axles, brakes, and wheels.

I'm alone and I'm aware of it, for the first time.
Alone in June, alone at the start of summer vacation,
alone with the summer wind, alone with the sweet song
of red-breasted robins, alone with the whirr of wound-up lawn mowers,
alone with the *whack* and *whap* of bats and balls down at the park.

My nostrils fill with the smell of freshly mowed grass,
my eyes smart with streaming sunlight, my fingertips warm
to the touch of just-sawed two-by-fours,
my thin arms sag under the weight of tools
hauled in from my dad's hand-made,
silver-painted workbench.

All at once —
in one swift moment—
I know I *know.*
I know I'm *knowing* I'm *alive*
and not *not* alive, not dead,
not like my recently deceased grandfather,
not unborn like our neighbor's nine stillborn babies.

It's too *crazy*, I'm thinking, as I move
in slow motion down the driveway,
too amazing to keep to myself, too cool
not to share it with Mark, who's now
shuffling across the Kocher's lawn
and heading straight to our go-kart.

I'm dying to tell him what's going on with me,
but can't even open my mouth, which feels stuck together
with peanut butter, chockfull of marbles, numb as a dentist-visit.
I'm weirded out by the word balloon rising over my head,
like the ones my dad reads to me from the funny papers,
but this one's doggone empty.
All I can manage is a petulant,
"Give me a push, will ya?"
and careen down the driveway
and out of sight.

The Quakers say we open our souls with silence.
My Gramma Dora once told me sometimes there's a song
in what we cannot say, and happy the boy that the sun shines on.
A dying poet deigned to say we may be defined by what we first forget.

Maybe, could be. All I know is what I know.
Everything I've said since that coruscating moment
on the sun-warmed driveway, under summer's scudding clouds,
is an effort to make up for that failure,
that inability to describe that miracle,
the thwarted soul force of that silence
that marked me for life
with the bittersweet destiny
of turning my world
into words,
my life
into
legend.

THE TIME OF THE GYPSIES

Years later,
I encountered them, tentatively,
on the back roads of many a far-flung land,
begging in the town square of Constanta, Romania,
selling tin dishes along the road in County Down,
bartering switchblades under the arches of the Roman Coliseum,
setting up leather tents in the cork fields of Portugal,
being hassled by Greek police at the crossroads to Delphi.

But the first time I met a real gypsy was in my own front yard,
and I've got proof, etched in black and white and printed on 3 x 3
Kodak paper, me, at three, on the back of a piebald pony
held by a marvelous stranger named "Two-fer."
That's what we neighborhood kids called the swarthy horse rider
in the multicolored scarves and vest, big black Spanish hat, and earrings,
who came to visit every spring with his long tall drink of a friend
who pulled the big-wheeled cart full of necklaces, beads, and love potions.
Every autumn they'd return with the cart full of pumpkins, gourds,
and dried flowers sprayed gold or silver for the holiday tables.
Every October, as the maple leaves fell like colored asterisks
on the browning grass of the front yard, the gypsies offered home repairs,
like sharpening our mother's knives on their whirring gray whetstone,
until they were sharp as Spanish swords, my mother bragged to her
rich sisters in Grosse Point and Birmingham.

The images baffle as they shine in my mind.
They sparkle like clear crystal water that hides a dangerous shoreline.
They glint like the very eyes of the stubble-chinned stranger
whose face grazed my arm as he lifted me on top of the pony,

and his brass hoop earrings glittered as he sang,
"Two rides for three dollars, two for three, two for three, ladies."

To this day, I wonder where our gypsies came from,
how on earth they ended up in a lily-white, post-war
American subdivision, "betwixt and between,"
as our mothers used to say,
half-way between Detroit and Chicago,
down the pike from the back of beyond,
eight thousand miles from exotic, god-intoxicated India,
four thousand miles from dear, dowdy Dublin,
a world away from wherever home was for
the "traveling people," those unlettered genius exiles
who learned to whisper sweet secrets
into the ears of their horses,
and the hearts of lonely housewives:
"Two fer three, ladies, two fer three.
A ride on a carousel or a pony will add
a year to your children's life, Ma'am."

How on earth will I ever know which years
are the ones those gypsy rides added on to my life?
If I knew, would I live them any differently?
When asked, the travelers say just ride the mystery.

FOR MY FATHER WHO NEVER MADE IT TO PARIS

for Richard Beban

For my father who never made it to Paris
I meet friends late at night in smoky cafes
To drink frothy cappuccinos and listen
To Coltrane sax solos on old jukeboxes
And talk of the wounds
Of fathers and sons.

For fathers and sons
Who never returned home,
I reach down for words to express my grief
Like an emergency ward surgeon groping
For stray shrapnel in the flesh
Of bleeding loved ones.

For all the words never found between men,
The buried burning words slowly infecting us,
I drop quarters in no-name telephones
To call suicidal friends, distraught young fathers,
Lone wolf sons who howl at the indifferent moon,
And offer the round table of brotherhood.

For all the tumors caused by sorrow,
And all the ulcers formed by anger,
For all the nightmares wrought by rage,
And all the emptiness carved by despair,
I probe friends and family
For healing stories.

For my father and all fathers
Who never saw Paris,
One friend listens, reveals,
Reaches into an open wound,
Finds a piece of gold shrapnel,
Cashes it in for airfare,
Takes his father
to the Left Bank.

So the healing
Can begin.

Paris
1986

LIGHTNING IN ST. CHAPELLE

After a sublime afternoon at the Musee d'Orsay
Puzzling together over Picasso's *Man with the Blue Guitar*,
We settle into the narrow pews of the king's relic-riddled chapel
Where the flute player blows sweetstrange notes
That hover in the candlelit air around us,
The lutist's fingers move across the strings
Like a weaver in the Gobelin tapestry factory,
And the tenor's voice reaches out to the heavens
To make music out of God's notable breath.
Suddenly, like the stroke that fells a giant oak,
A thunderclap stuns the stone.
Lightning cuts a hole through
The dark cape of Parisian night.
Bolts of burnt yellow and searing green
Flash across the arching poems of stained-glass windows
And the last song shimmers like the voices of monks
Admonishing pilgrims leaving for Jerusalem
To keep their eyes on heaven.
You turn and wrap your loving arms around me
Like a benediction, reminding me
How two hearts
Might sing
As one,
Yet.

THE KNOCK

Not for all the tea in China,
Not for all the cigars in Cuba,
Not for all the cars in Detroit,

Would I trade the knock
That came from the other side
Of the door.

Not for all the moose in Canada,
Not for all the coals in Newcastle,
Not for all the baseballs in Cooperstown.

Not for what I saw
When I opened the door.
Not for that first glance

Of your utterly
Lovely
Face.

THE SCULPTOR

He is grieving by the sea, wiping away briny tears
with marble-dusted hands. The sudden squall
whips the waves into a froth of anger.
The cargo ship carrying his bronze victory statue
of the brave sprinter, Skamandros of Mitylene,
flails in the mighty swells, its masts teetering,
the ship slipping irretrievably below the water,
then sinking like a soul banished to the netherworld,
the bottom of the vengeful sea.
No wonder they say Poseidon is the only god
who never laughs, the one who takes his revenge
on mortals for reasons they may never know,
he cries to himself, falling to his knees,
Years of my life, years of my life . . . .
The thought of his best work lost
forever cuts like a Spartan sword.
I used to think, he tells himself, *it doesn't matter*
if anyone outside Olympia ever sees my work
for all that matters is the pleasure of the gods.
That was the infinite moment,
As the poet said, he realized
why he was not allowed to sign his work.
His statues were meant to be as breathtaking
as the athletes themselves.
How else is excellence preserved,
his mentor challenged him,
but in song, in stone, in metal?
Show some ingenuity, boy,
make the bronze runners *breathe*

64

with spirit, make them *move*
with courage, make them *sing*
with joy, and your work
will make the gods weep
with envy.

IV

The deeper blue becomes, the more urgently it summons man
toward the infinite, the more it arouses in him a longing
for purity, and, ultimately, for the supersensual. . . .
[blue is] the infinite penetration
into the absolute essence.
　　　　　—— *Wassily Kandinsky*

PROTEUS

What startles me about the shape-shifting son of Poseidon is how the slippery god was banished to the rocky edge of the watery world beneath the surface of all things. He learned to hide from the world of mortals because he held divine secrets they would die for. When Menelaus and his shipwrecked crew discovered that the soothsaying son lived alone below the sea and emerged but once a day, at noon, the hour of Pan, to sun himself on the rocks, they risked everything to wrestle with him on the treacherous rocks. They'd heard from old sailors that if Proteus was caught by mere mortals he had to answer any questions they asked of him — the secret of the winds, wave, cloud and bird-flight patterns, sea-changes — the way home for long lost warriors.

But divine knowledge does not come easily. So great were the secrets of the gods, his father taught him how to protect them by transforming himself — through a wild whirlwind of motion into tiger, serpent or centaur to avoid being captured and reveal what no man should know, the unbearable burden of the unassimilable future.

This was the mythical road home for homesick sailors, through the portals of advice of the god of change, via the advice of the god the soul, who alone knows the way home. Only the Old Man of the Sea can help shipwrecked souls, those who have sacrificed everything and have nothing left to lose. Spirit is the wind that carries us along, but soul is the compass that sends us back to the center of everything. It's our desire for home that allows us to wrestle our monsters on the jagged stones of our lost, slippery hours. That desire is the keystone to the arch of mystery curving over the storm of your longing for change that will get you home again.

wind -essay

69

THE WAY OF THE WORLD

By the time the old archivist turned 160 years old, he'd grown weary of the corruption of the ruling class in palace life. No one listened anymore to the wisdom of the old ways. They scoffed at the wisdom he'd winnowed from the most venerable books left behind by the ancestors. There was only one thing that would bring him peace of mind. Like the Taoist masters before him, he had to leave the velvet cage of the Middle Kingdom and spend his remaining years in the hardscrabble mountain life far to the west.

The old man quietly left late one night under a sceptered moon, riding in a rickety chariot pulled by a lumbering black ox. This would be his last journey. He rolled on for many days through the dangerous trail called the Han-Ku Pass. When he finally reached the last border gate, he was unceremoniously stopped by a young soldier named Yin His, the Keeper of the Pass, who claimed to be less than surprised by his arrival. The border guard had been reading the clouds, watching the flight of birds, counting the rainfall. The omens predicted everything. "You are about to withdraw yourself, from sight," he said, knowingly. "I pray you compose a book for me."

The wizened sage pulled at his white beard, adjusted the reins of his chariot. He had not expected this. He knew that whatever he said would not be the way, that the way of the world could not be said. Have faith in the way things are, he wanted to say, the way is the way of *wu wei*, the way of not doing but being. It took him 5,000 characters to not say so, in a work compiled by the Keeper of the Pass, later called the *Tao Te Ching*, and credited to the "Old Man," Lao Tzu.

The old sage could not *not* have known this. He shrugged his shoulders, adjusted his courtly robes, and left for the farthest reaches of the west, rolling where there was no where there. The Keeper of the Pass told those that followed that the old man's chariot wheels left no tracks, no way.

MOUNTAIN MAN

The starched shirt city folk from the Tennessee Valley Authority, well, they just didn't get it. They couldn't comprehend why the old codger wouldn't budge from his dilapidated log cabin, couldn't figure out why he wouldn't settle for a suitcase full of cash, the promise of a brand spanking new cabin in the next hollar, or a new rifle, a better rocking chair, a faster hunting dog. "Don't you get it?" they asked him, "*Progress*, the dream of a better life than th—?" As long as he dawdled on that porch, sucking on that corncob pipe, swigging from that old clay jug at his feet, they agreed, the new dam wouldn't ever be built.

"*What would it take for you to move?*" the exasperated engineer asked the old mountain man as the bulldozers snarled like attack dogs, and the stiff-necked accountants double-checked their figures. But the grizzled old fellah just kept shaking his shock of long white hair, ignoring him like a bad cold, or a rude tax collector.

"Don't 'spose y'all'd like to glug some shine?" the mountain man drawled, deliberately like someone used to measuring his words in shot glasses. "Nah, didn't think so. Well, then, I'd be obliged if y'all come inside and sit a spell." He ratcheted up and out of his chair, launching a long stream of chaw right past their shiny Florsheims, leaving a bold brown asterisk on the ground. "I'm gonna give ya some truth, gonna show you why y'all came down the hard road for nuthin'."

The engineer grimaced and stormed inside, scuffing his shoes on the beaten dirt floor of the cabin as he shuffled nervous-like past the wooden table, three-legged stool, and narrow bed, and stood before the burning fireplace. "My grandpappy lit this here fire over one hundred years ago, he said softly, but determinedly, through his teeth. My pappy kept it lit. I've kept it lit. Never gone out. You wanna know why I ain't movin. 'Cuz of that there fire. If I goes out, it goes out. That's why I ain't movin'. Nah, that dog won't hunt."

Next day, the hollars saw one of the strangest sights since that flouncy English songcatcher went poking her nose around the valley asking the local music folk to talk into her recordin' box. The engineer directed the wheezing bulldozer to sink its iron teeth deep into the holy ground right smack underneath the mountain man's teetering cabin, then hoist the cabin high into the warm Tennessee sky, with the blood red earth and the family fire intact, and drop it soft as a baby into its cradle, all nice and easy-like on the smoke-belching flatbed truck.

Under a copper-colored sky and blue moon rising, the moving truck moseyed down the switchback roads with the mountain man, cabin, and fire together, bumping and bucking on the hardpan roads. They drove past the swiftly flowing river, round hardscrabble towns, and down to the distant valley where the mountain man settled in, and tended his ancestral fire till the day, as they say in these parts, he done died.

He went out before the fire did, which is the way he wanted it. He knew better than most. One false move, the fire goes out.

TRACKING

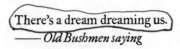

There's a dream dreaming us.
—— *Old Bushmen saying*

After a long day of filming I can't sleep. I catch the last shuttle heading through the eerily silent streets of Cape Town to the Harbor Mall where I'm hoping to find a late-night souvenir stand and get a present for my son. Shuffling along, I find myself tracking the sounds of clinking glasses and a soccer game on television. Telltale signs of a waterhole in the cold desert of the urban night.

Suddenly, a commotion breaks out, high-pitched laughter, squeals of delight, followed by soft commands in the strange *clicking* language of the Bushmen from the South African interior. They're an uncanny sight. A band of hunters in bare feet, leather loincloths, steenbok skins, traditional bows slung across their shoulders, hunting bags in hand. The elders move stealthily across the linoleum-tiled floor, quietly studying the ancient language of footprints left behind by the stuffed animals in the window of the local travel agency. They gesture to the young ones trailing behind, who are circling a kiosk stuffed with wooden animal sculptures. With uncanny mimicry, the elders cry out to the impalas, leopards, and elephants. Voices from the desert, shadowy figures from the far-flung African past.

I raise my dummy-proof camera to capture a glorious moment that seems to have emerged from the dawn of the world, but can't bring myself to pull the trigger. The old men hunch now in the center of the mall, as if in nighttime consultation deep in the desert. I hear their distinctive, telegraph-like *clicks*. One of them turns to me. I imagine him to be a medicine man. He has proud cheekbones and fearless eyes that have stared down lions. He locks eyes with my long camera lens. For a flickering

74

moment the hunter is the hunted. He is a vulnerable gazelle staring down a loaded rifle, contemplating imminent death. He sees his reflection in the polished lens, just this side of persuasion. The baffled kids are scratching at the window, wondering why the gazelles do not move, why the lion does not roar. They laugh, uneasily, stick out their tongues, daringly, half-hoping the animals will leap through the window and their hunt will resume. Down the hall a janitor kicks over a bucket — and the band of terrified kids bolts away, as if chased by wild jackals across the hot sands of the Kalahari.

I'm imagining the old man thinking, *It's true, as the old ones said. None of this is happening. The world is dreaming us.* That's why I can't pull the trigger. You can't bring a photo back from a dream.

If I move somebody might wake up; it could be me. ——

POSTCARD FROM MENORCA

Over the Spanish cafe ritual of perfumado, coffee and anis and a host of postcards, journals and papers and crackling shortwave radio, I practice the gentle and venerable art of travel, acknowledging the mystery of movement across the world, a planchette sliding across a Ouija board, or a Dutch skater gliding over a frozen canal. By this act of attention and compression I can send home a simple, if idealized picture that provides a little evidence that I've tasted a slice of blue heaven, drunk from a pitcher of paradise.

Do I send winged cards to convince myself I actually did travel somewhere, was moved by moving? Or do I select and emboss them with my collected impressions to enchant someone who appreciates the transport of an exotic stamp, genuine enthusiasm, a well-turned phrase that captures the *perfume*, the savor, the relish of time, the smack and tang of someplace more real than the unreality of home?

No. I am alone here in search of happiness. I'm trying to reach out to you from the bare bones of things, "grubbing happily for words," as D. H. Lawrence said, practicing what my Italian friends call *dolce far niente*, the simple art of being happy in the moment. In these palm-sized poems I'm sharing with you how the world astounds me with simple marvels, like the sight of tonight's white-handed stars rising over the distant pine forest. Spelling this out to you, half a world away, proves I'm not alone, that I'm connected across the world, if only on the wings of these far-flung words, if only by the transport of ecstatic observations.

ARS LONGA, VITA BREVIS

The Venerable Bede, a seventh-century philosopher, lamented the brevi-
ty of life, but in the same breath praised the long light we leave behind.
During one of his illuminating lucubrations he compared human existence to the night flight of a bird through total darkness that suddenly
enters the door of a brightly lit hall, wings its way through, and exits out
the other end, returning to the darkness from which it came. Today we
would miss the metaphor and notice only the speed of escape.

"Follow the light," the photographer Ansel Adams told his students.
"That's all you need to remember, just follow the light." In the sanctuary of his darkroom overlooking the glittering Carmel coast he turned
darkness into light. Now we've lost the luxuriousness of that *slow* time
inside the darkroom, notice only the waste of time, reach for our instru-
ments of instant gratification. "Send me some light—I need it bad," Elvis
used to mutter under his breath and over his flopsweat, moments before
going on stage to perform, "I'm afraid I'll go out like a light, just like I
came on." The dream of light, remarked Springsteen. "It's like Elvis came
along and whispered a dream in everyone's ear, and then we all dreamed
about it somehow."

"In the deep dark he alone sees the light," wrote Chuang Tzu from his
mountain retreat, in the manner of Tung-pin Lu, "the light itself is *the*
creative." Every second, the cosmologist Brian Swimme reminded the
shuttered class, the sun burns four million tons of itself to create light.
Everything you do depends on that cosmic generosity. *If that isn't enough
to be grateful, then what is?* he asked, laughing, radiantly. Oh, light, eighth
wonder of the world, shine on us in our darkest hour.

[handwritten marginalia: sun going down — Shines with a zeal, a ferocity / its last chance of the day to pierce the heart / some enter mine / how nice]

[handwritten marginalia: Blue quotes too few]

77

Today the floes came . . .
A blue light glowed from their crevices.
They might have been souls.
—— *Mary Oliver*

THE FIRST LAW OF CONSERVATION

So I'm busy telling tall tales to old friends
around the old beer barrel table at O'Reilly's Pub,
which is why I never notice my little boy dipping
his tiny hand into my precious pint of Guinness,
swirling his fingers around like stir sticks,
and laughing as the creamy foam spills
over the edge of the dark glass.
Suddenly, an Irish lad with a face so white
it counts as a County Donegal rain tan,
reaches across our table and grabs my son's hand
like a lollipop and sticks the whole thing
into his parched mouth, scaring my poor boy half to death,
at least until the little guy yanks his fingers out with a *pop*
that sounds like a cork leaping out of a champagne bottle.
The young Irishman feels our eyes raking him
for some kind of explanation, his face as red
as Connemara salmon, and lets loose
with a loud smack of his lips, explaining,
"Me mum used to say, 'Laddie, never waste a drop.'"
Well, it's hard to argue with such a bonafide piece of wisdom,
especially considering the unvarnished fact
that he hadn't been served yet,
and the thirst for the Irish holy water was upon him.
But then we had to explain to our crying blue boy
why he couldn't play with his own pint,
like all the other lads.
"Soon enough, lad," sighed Seamus, "soon enough."

THE OLDEST LIVING PERSON IN THE WORLD

She was born in 1875, the year before Alexander Graham Bell
invented the telephone, ten years before the spidery ironwork
of the Eiffel Tower rose over the Seine. She said she was fifteen
when she noticed Van Gogh wandering around her hometown of Arles
searching for azure blue skies and absinthe green drinks
when he should've been looking for soap. She and her husband
survived the widow-maker First World War, but during the Second Slaught
when she reached her sixties, she lost him and her only daughter.
When she turned 121, she recorded a rap record called "Time's Mistress."
By then, Madame Calmant, the Oracle of Arles,
was known far and wide for admonishing visitors who came to her
for advice about how to live a long life.
"*Ne quittez pas.*" "Don't worry,"
she snapped at them, which worried them even more,
since they were French, which is shorthand for stress.
"If you can't do anything about it," she insisted,
"Don't worry about it."
The remark sent a *frisson* down the spine of the Académie Français.
In a *panique*, they convened a special session entitled,
"On the Impossibility of Living a Worry-Free Existence."
On the eve of her 126th, and last, birthday party,
Madame was flattered by a reporter from *Le Monde* about her
remarkably clear complexion and worry-free demeanor,
to which she replied with *l'esprit d'escalier,*
"I've never had but *one* wrinkle —
and I'm sitting on it."

THE STRANGE FLOW OF SYNCHRONICITY

Mama told me money didn't grow on trees.
Papa talked a blue streak to me about the way he blew it,
Adding, contritely, that I better hold onto it because it had wings
And would fly out of my pockets as if it had a mind of its own.
All this came to mind the night I was scribbling some notes
For my screenwriting class about the use and misuse
Of coincidence in the movies, red-penciling a scene
From Martin Scorcese's *After Hours*, the riotous one
Where the benighted hero flags down a cab at two in the morning
So he can meet up with a sultry waitress he'd met in an all-night diner.
The second he climbs into the cab a chance gust of wind
Snatches the poor fool's last twenty-dollar bill out of his hand
And flings it out the open window across the cobbled streets
Of Greenwich Village, through the open door of the waitress's apartment
Then out again across the city that never sleeps, and into a wormhole
Of time where it appears again on the pages of my class outline.
That's the moment I heard my name shouted, "Phil! Phil!"
And looked up to see Jim, an old friend from my Detroit factory years
Striding towards me with a wall-to-wall grin, triumphantly
Holding a twenty-dollar bill high in the coffee-scented air.
"Cous! Man, I was just walking down the street telling my friends
About you when I saw this twenty-spot on the sidewalk.
I bent down to pick it up and when I stood back up, man,
I saw you sitting here writing in your notebook.
So, I've just *gotta know*, what were you working on
Just now when I walked through the door?"

P PAINTER

ı these murky spyglass windows,
luted frames sanded raw
By my own see-sawing hands,
I try to see beyond this workadaddy world
Of paint-scabbed, caulk-pussed,
Spackle-rashed tarps stretched taut
As the sails on the bay below,
Try to think beyond the life
Betrayed by my painter's overalls that stand up
By themselves in the corner of the garage
When we lock up 'round midnight
After another soul-numbing
Sixteen-hour painting binge,
To a future that doesn't include
Renovating whorescoped, har-di-har-harlotted,
Victorian mansions for the more Frisco-than-thou crowd.

While crabbed clouds scuttle across the sky
I add a fourth coat of gentian blue to the window sash,
Praying I'm not painting over my own future,
Hope against hope that my fever-blistered hands
Aren't just gilding the San Frantasia lily,
Aren't turning me into a pimp-poet
Who's selling the muse's gifts
To any john cruising
The Yellow Pages
Who's willing to pay
By the stroke of paint,
By the thrust of caulk,
By the caress of sanding.

"Ya gotta believe,"
   the ballplayer said to himself
   as he strode to the mound
   in the bottom of the ninth
   of the seventh game of the World Series,
   though no one else believed in him,
   and I've gotta believe
   I'm buying myself
   a pimp mobile of
   bad-ass freedom,
   which is why
   I'm cultivating
   this holy fool smile
   on the scaffolding
   this afternoon.

I'm four stories above the street,
and one story away from
the rest of my life.

January, 1980

SANDING

Sanding away the ego,
Scraping away the id,
Spackling away the superego.
Patching up the perforated
Holes of the past,
Caulking the cracks between
Present, past and future,
Time reveals itself
In the eternal grain of wood
Behind the palimpsest of painter's tricks
Layered like changing opinions
That gloss over underlying truths.
The house painter is a *poèt manque*
Who longs to uncover the depths
Beneath the veneer,
Dares to delve for timeless truths
Below the fleeting news of the day,
As the poet is a *peintre manque*
Who dares to expose the grain of raw reality,
The nerves that run through all wood,
Then lays down word-colors
To make life shine
With epiphanies of paint.

September, 1983

SEMAPHORES OF SEDUCTION

She slides across the floor of the hair salon
Sneaking flirtatious glances over her rolling shoulder,
Her lips wet with amorous anticipation,
Her red finger-nailed hands signaling for me like flags
In semaphores of sweet seduction.

I slip wearily into the soft leather chair,
And put my feet up on the steel footrest.
She changes the radio to KJAZ, starts to sway
To the bebopping rhythms of Dexter Gordon,
Snapping her fingers and spinning me around
In the barber chair as if leading in a swing dance routine.
At first I resist, my neck stiffening, and she backs away,
Now humming the melody to "Night Train,"
With her eyes closed, and so I fall,
Contented, into her hands, which hover over
The shampoo sink, where the warm water
Is magically running, and soon she is tugging
my hair, running warm water through it,
lathering me with long, searching fingers,
then rinsing me with hot water and warm words.

To an Ella Fitzgerald blues number, the hair stylist,
As she refers to herself, lifts up my head and cradles me
In the sauna of heat between her breasts,
Which leave a steamy imprint on my tingling scalp
As she slowly dries my hair with a warm towel and cooing sounds.
Spinning me around again, this time to face the wall-to-wall mirror,

She cuts and shears, clips and shorns, asks my sign,
My workout schedule, my diet, what kind of car I drive,
Where I live, where I go skiing during the winter
[Tahoe or Mammoth?] and where I want to go when I die.
While holding a fleck of beige paint between those blazing red fingernails,
she asks me what I *really* do, well,
when I'm not *house-painting*.

"Well, I'm really a writer," I say, dreading the idea
of explaining why I'm spending more time with my hands
on a paintbrush than a typewriter.
"Writer?" she gasps, dropping her hand to her heaving bosom.
"Why, I can't write my own name!"

I am just about to launch into my
"Everybody's a writer" routine,
when she freezes, scissors poised before my eyes, says,
"But I can *dance*, at least, when I'm inspired.
Maybe that's why I've never really felt the *need*
To write, cuz I dance when I feel like I have something to say!"
She glows like a Yosemite sunrise with the sudden realization.
Her cheeks flush, her lips form the word *write*,
Her eyes stare at the glint of steel blades
Like she's never really noticed the cutting beauty before.
Her forehead furls in bewilderment as she catches
Her own reflection in the mirror.
Softly, I say, "I guess I dance with my fingers
And you write with your feet."
"Yeah, yeah, that's it, that's *it!*" she sighs,
grateful for the vote of confidence, blissful from the blessing

from on high, and then slowly pulls my wandering head
back into the safe harbor between her now
sweating B-movie starlet breasts.

"I ain't ever thought of it like that."

San Francisco
1988

SARASOTA'S TRUE BEACHCOMBERS

Back and forth they go,
        Down the beach,
Heads down, looking for signs
        Of life, shapes of beauty,
Signs from the depths
        Of the sea, signals
Of transcendent life,
        Whorls of force,
Any life at all in this dead
        And dying place,
Where the snowbirds come
        To live out their wintry discontent
But showing few signs of life,
        Leaving behind no tracks,
Dropping dead in the
        Middle of nowhere.
Back and forth they go,
        Twenty-four little sandpipers
Marching down the beach,
        Two dozen tiny poets
Searching for ways to survive,
        Beaked heads bobbing side to side,
Eyes ceaselessly darting,
        Looking for life to skewer
With the piercing word so
        They might keep the species alive.

UNDER A MANGO MOON

Under the sheen
of Iba's keen blue skies,
scalloped waves slip over
lagoon reefs of fluted coral
onto palm-fringed beaches
where nut-brown boys
with horseshoe smiles ·
cheerfully load brightly
painted outrigger canoes
with glistening fishing nets
and dull gray sticks
of dynamite.

At dusk, under a mango moon,
they set sail with their fathers,
calmly trusting wind, waves,
clouds, and birds, and old sea
stories to lead them to the bounty below.

The explosives they drop
on the coral reefs are meant
only to stun the fish, they tell
their mothers at dawn when
huddling inside the nipa huts,
and are asked why the catch,
again, has been so poor.

SAME, SAME SAIGON

The quiet outdoor café is just what we were looking for,
A last vestige of the sleepy rhythms of colonial life,
Worlds away from the expat revelry of the Apocalypse Now disco,
The sell-you-my-sister bartering at The Heart of Darkness bar,
And the Miss Saigon pageant of prostitutes riding
The latest Italian scooters around the town square.
After running the bawdy Saigon steeplechase
My brother and I have found an easy-going hangout
For locals who just appreciate good local food,
Which is what we expected when the blue-frocked waiter
Tries to explain to us, first in elegant French, then in clipped German,
And finally in staccato English, that the long menu page
Of crisply photographed rice plates were,
"Same, same, but different ... same, same, but different ... "
Shrugging, we order randomly, unable to read a word,
But able to enjoy the spectacular coconut-curries that come our way.
After lunch, we shamble on over to a nearby rare book shop
Whose display window features three mahogany bookshelves,
Each one covering a separate war. The shelves are labeled
In classical Vietnamese script with English subtitles:
The Chinese War, The French War, and *The American War.*
The grisly photographs of dead soldiers
On each book cover look the same,
The same, but
Different.

January, 1996

IF YOU TRAVEL

If you travel far enough
There will come a day
When you recognize yourself
Coming down the road

And you'll cross the street
To avoid the collision

If you travel long enough
There will come a day
When you hear yourself
Catching up

And you'll slow down to gawp
At what you were trying
In vain to avoid
All along

If you stay home,
you'll miss out on
these strange dancing
lessons from God

BOOKCASE

What moved me most
About Anne Frank's ill-fated house
Along the canals of Amsterdam,
Wasn't the photographs of Auschwitz,
But something deceptively, achingly ordinary.

The whole world knows by now
How the precociously sensitive teenage girl
Lived here secretly for two years with her family
Before being betrayed by some still-unknown character.
Whether a neighbor, a friend, a customer, no one knows.

Before visiting the hideaway I'd always wondered
How her father and uncle came and went,
Silent as church mice, anxious as criminals,
Without alerting the Nazi raiders who were
Filling their trains of doom with Jews.

Then I saw the movable bookcase,
Nailed together out of scrap wood,
Its shelves filled with business ledgers,
Its swivel hinges hidden from view,
The narrow wooden switchback staircase
Behind it, all but invisible, the twisted
Life of silent meals, terror-laced sleep,
All but unimaginable.
In a novel this would be a magical bookcase,
A staircase of marvels leading to an inner sanctum,
A miraculous construction out of Holmes, Eco or Borges,

Leading to a garden of forking paths, a library of babel,
A treasure trove of Euripides' hundred missing plays,
Aristotle's lost comedies.

But this was no imaginary bookcase.
It opened on to a train with no windows,
A camp with no mercy, a gas chamber
With no chance for escape.
This bookcase contained no miraculous volumes
That revealed the map of their redemption,
Nor the dark truth of their fate.

Still, the girl managed to write
Late one night that she still believed
"in the goodness of the human race,"
Words that would outlive her
And put a lovely face
With far-seeing green eyes,
On the fearsome anonymity,
The numbing numbers,
The six million dead,
For which the world
Would forgive God
Too soon.

HIROSHIMA

I'm staring earnestly at the stone-koan-of-a-boulder
in the Kyoto temple garden, trying to meditate
on the meaning of a menacing tiger
lurking within the rock,
when I hear the troubled voice of a tour guide.
She is walking past the garden to the tea house
in the distant pine grove, a blue-kimonoed,
white-powder-faced woman who reminds
me of a pilgrim in a Hokusai painting.
She is speaking bitterly to a young tourist,
who shakes her head in distress and mumbles
Hai! as she tries to sympathize.

I am trying not to write about this.

I am trying not to remember how ashamed
I felt for eavesdropping, and tried in vain to turn
my attention back to the elusive stone tiger.
But their strange words were carried to me
as if I were meant to hear them.
"One of my clients wants to see the street in Hiroshima
where the white flashes burned people's shadows
into the cement like X-rays," gasped the tour guide.
"What do I tell her? I do not want to be rude, but — "
The stunned tourist puts her hand to her mouth.
"That's sick," she says, "why would anyone
want to see such a thing?"

The two women pause
on the stone path
to watch the dark flight
of a murder of crows.
The guide speaks in a voice
as plaintive as last night's rain
on the cobbled garden paths.

"How can you see what can't be seen anymore?"

She winces, as if struck
by the blunt memory of the bomb's
sudden flare of white light, tightens her grip
on the handle of her imperial blue umbrella.
She gestures towards the blazing sun,
then down to the path beneath
her wooden sandals, her
face full of *mono aware*,
the slender sadness,
the world-weary sigh
that permeates the
ancient future.

THE WINDY WALLS OF TROY

Long gone, but never far away, you're still at my side.
Maybe even more than ever before, I'm thinking as I step
Through the stone-toothed gates of Homer's Troy, where,
Legend has it, the Greeks rolled the Trojan Horse, a stout-
Hearted story we read together when I was a boy
And you were the age I am now.

The slanted thirty-three-hundred year-old walls
Rise into view like the sides of a stone pool from underwater.
Suddenly I can't breathe and reel with vertigo
Prompted by the phantom touch of
Your hand on my shoulder, the ghostly
Echo of your book-strengthened voice

assoc w/ grief

Hectoring me to dig deep for the roots of everything,
"Otherwise you'll never know what you're talking about, son.
And you don't want that, do you?"
No, dad, I mumble, as I gaze across
The Trojan plains to the faraway sea,
I don't want that.

just 1 d
BP
notes like
to feel like
I don't know

As I make my first circuit around the siege-thickened walls,
I wonder against wonder if this can really be the site of
The mythic ten-year battle that has haunted me all my life,
As if the war somehow mirrored those in own life,
And it's then I hear the roar of wild boar regret
In my thickly forested heart that you didn't live
Long enough to journey here with me and be stunned by the electric blue
Morning glories growing in the crevices of the ancient

Roman theater, or hear the water pumps in the distant fields
Where local guides have told wayward pilgrims for centuries

That Achilles, "the swift runner," was buried,
Or finger the very dirt in the trenches dug by that rogue hero
Of yours, the archaeologist Heinrich Schliemann, or debate
The new breed of scientists from the University of Cincinnati —
Oh, but that would've warranted a lecture on the origins of the word

Cincinnati, and a hot debate about the nine layers of Troy,
Arguments which would've echoed the multiple levels
Of our own unfathomable relationship.
But you never left home.
Now I travel the world for both of us,
Wondering every step of the way,
If someday my own son

Will war with me or fight alongside me,
A story that has played out since the days these walls fell,
Sending men on life-long voyages to find their own way home again.

We gave up on each
Other too soon.

Troy, Turkey
1990

SHADOW BOXES

On their long trek across the blue-veined glaciers
of Thule, Greenland, the vagrant Viking explorers
Knud Rasmussen and Peter Freuchen searched
for a missing *anagok*, a medicine woman
wise in the ways of her people, who had last
been seen trapping fox in the distant north.

"So there you are," Semagak said, when they
found her trapped inside an ice-bound cave.
The old conjurer was huddled deep within the skin
of the only fox she'd killed, and told them she'd been
expecting them because the spirits of her dead ancestors
reassured her two white men from another world
were coming to save her.

Semagak spent that infernally long white winter with the explorers
As they hunted for the most elusive of arctic animals,
Eskimo songs, myths, folklore, and hunting tales.
She knitted, cooked, cleaned, and told stories meant to ward off
the claws of black dog darkness and blue dog depression.
One day while snow piled in twenty-foot drifts
around their cabin and their breath turned to ice crystals,
she went beserk, smashing their cameras against their dogsled
saying her songs were not being taken seriously.

During the blue-boned blizzard, Rasmussen
discovered Semagak's secret collection of boxes and bags
that she'd been storing away for some unknown reason.

"I collect shadows and darkness," she said,
"so that the world will get light again,
and I keep it all locked up there in these boxes."

*

One balmy winter evening in Berkeley
as I collected my notes after a weekend workshop
a student cornered me, and earnestly asked,
"Why do you have to tell such dark stories,
like that creepy myth of Sisyphus, or show
such downer movies, like Joyce's *The Dead*,
or read such depressing poetry,
like Rilke's 'Sonnets to Orpheus'"?
"It's so *Sixties*," she said, increasingly annoyed.
"You know, there's just, kinda, you know,
enough darkness already."

Recollecting the warning sign
I once noticed on the door
of a famous animation room:

If you open this door
the darkness
will leak out.

I said, "Be careful what you ask for.
Do you remember this afternoon's story
about the Eskimo shaman?
Do you remember what Rasmussen reported?"

The student shrugged, feigning boredom.
"After watching her collect the darkness
For three straight winters, Rasmussen concluded,
'Every spring, sure enough,
the sun came back.'"

Carefully filing away the last of my class
notes into my leather satchel,
I slung the road-burnished bag
over my shoulder and thought,
I need a very long journey.

With a much-practiced moue
curling around her mouth, she said,
"Why can't you lighten up?"

But I don't believe she meant it.

EARTHBONES

The aborigines say when you die you go sky,
when you in trouble you go forward
into outback, you dig up your stone
you bury it where no one can find
it but you, and before you don't
know it, you'll be out of
trouble. Or so says
the dreamtime
painter, to me
on the Sydney
docks,
a ritual
I can dig,
down to the
depths of my soul
that, he says, as we journey
toward the ruined world, looking
for clues to restore our perdurable
secrets. Yes, the aborigines say when
you die you go sky, but I don't know,
I only know when you live your sapphire
blue soul is flung like an earthbone boomeranging
from one world to another and back again, over and over.

FRETTING

The worrisome dream returns at dawn,
the one with me fingering the frets
of a blazingly blue guitar,
making old-timey
foot-tapping music
until some clown in the audience points out
there aren't any strings on my guitar —
which throws me into a panic —
so I press harder, pretending
to bend notes like B. B. King
the night he found his thrill was gone
but hear
nothing
but the riffing rasps of my fingertips,
nothing but the echo of my playing
like there's no tomorrow,
like this is the only way
for me to lay my burden down
which is how I wake up,
in the Reverie Café,
listening to the plangent beat of rain
on the dirty window pane,
thinking, gratefully,
You're all worked up over nothing
but at least you're making music
out of your fretting

THE OLDEST WORDS IN ENGLISH, CORNWALL, 1980

By the tempered light coming
Through the leaded glass window
Of a three-hundred-year-old pub,
I read in a *Sunday Telegraph* article
that some clever linguists have determined
the four oldest words in the English
language: *gold, tin, apple, bad.*

It's enough to make a soul wonder
about the words I heard later that night,
the ones that set my hair on end,
the line uttered by the young swain
in the selfsame tavern, as he leaned
across the old oak bar, whispering
to the sultry barmaid,
I put the gold apples
in the bad tin,
love.

Maybe he read the same article I did,
or maybe it's the oldest line
in the oldest book
of love.

SPIDER WEBS

> And since I have seen these things
> I have been very conversant with spiders.
> — *Jonathan Edwards*

Unusually rested, I rise,
at dawn, in a prayerful mood.
Sweet morning light pours like butterscotch
through the wood frame window,
which I crank open slowly
in order to savor the moment,
like the subtlest tea.
It's only then, moving, thinking, feeling slowly,
that I see the silvery spider web stretched
across two panes of glass, a silken trap spun
through the night while the world slept.
      Tentatively,
I run my fingers along the springy pathways,
which glisten in the sunbeams, stringy filaments
that can withstand gale force winds, sticky
enough to hold fast the doomed prey
that the spider is now sailing towards
with "deathless pleasure."
      Rapturously,
I watch while an old nature documentary
drones on in my mind, its narration
motivating me to reach for my dictionary to look up
spinnaret , one of those museum words,
rarely seen but fortunately preserved,
letters and sounds that evoke the fluted fingerlike organs
of web-spinning orb-weavers who throw
runways, sailways, and balloonways,

draglines, rappel lines, and fly-trap lines,
shuddering strands for airborne creatures
who spin mile-long webs across mountains,
oceans, cellars, attics, and those dreadful
dungeon doorways that help creep out
every harum-scarum horror flick ever
flung at benumbed matinee audiences.
      Ludically,
I think of wild spider food
gossamer webs, luminous lines,
strand for strand stronger than steel,
filament by filament more luminous than light,
everywhere the web of life,
the "spider's paradisal spin,"
turning their readymade homes
into silvery trap of golden threads,
of beauty and horror,
side by side, strand by strand.
      Elliptically,
I think of my soul as a spider
weaving a web of words to catch its prey with prayer,
stretching, connecting, trapping everything in sight
with filaments of gossamer words, aloft
on my insatiable journey.

BLUISH

The old *babushka* confided to me in hushed tones
the rooms of the Fountain House I was visiting
had been turned into "The House of Curious Science"
after the carnage of the 1917 Revolution.
When the cabinets of wonder were emptied
for lack of interest and funds,
the fabled poet Anna Akhmatova
settled into these very rooms in the west wing
where she wrote her sad requiems of terror,
her soaring lyrics of endurance.

During the Yezhov terror, the elderly guide said,
the poet spent seventeen months waiting in line outside
the St. Petersburg prison waiting for even a glimpse
of her incarcerated husband.
One brutally cold afternoon
a poor peasant woman recognized her
as the poet of Mother Russia,
known in cellars, salons and cabarets
from the Kremlin to Siberia.
Later, the poet wrote,

A woman with bluish lips standing behind me, who,
of course, had never heard me called by name before,
woke up from the stupor to which everyone
had succumbed and whispered in my ear
[everyone spoke in whispers there]:
"Can you describe this?"
And I answered: "Yes, I can."

Then something that looked like a smile
passed over what had once been her face.

Akhmatova's supernatural confidence in the sacred duty of poets
to say the unsayable underscored her legend,
inspiring clandestine evenings in smoke-curdled rooms,
besiged by admirers who watched her drinking coffee
"as black as the slinky dresses she wore to recite her verse."

Rather than risk committing her poems to paper,
she committed them to memory, demanding
everyone who heard her poems learn them
by heart, so they might crisscross the vast land
conveying her verses to all who attended
in a kind of poet's telegraph system,
which she later reassembled.

The old *babushka* set down her knitting needles,
tugged on my sleeve as I tried leaving, leaned
forward, out of the long habit of suspicion.
Her dark bristled chin rubbed my cheek raw
as she rasped in vodka-scented English,
"What we learn by heart learns about us."
If it isn't a Russian proverb,
it should be.

cover

SIREN CALL

The creamy-colored Amazon river pours
into the dark black coffee of the Rio Negra.
Thunder tumbles down from frowning skies,
lightning scissors through crepe paper clouds,
a needling rain stings the luxuriant forest.
I stand alone on the bow of an old wooden riverboat
gazing spellbound through my funneled hands
at a shocking pink dolphin swimming alongside us,
breathing spumes of soft mist through the puckered opening
of her blowhole, her sleek dorsal fin cutting through
the turbid water like a spoon through cappuccino.
Then she dives and is gone, like a wisp of dream
we are unsure had ever visited us.

With her vanishing, the slashing rains are gone,
and the sun is back, glittering on the river
like a spray of diamonds, then slowly blistering
the green river world, bringing on the unsettling stillness.
The rickety boat putters along, the captain half-asleep,
the pilot putting his finger to his lips, pointing to the bare-
chested paddlers in canoes, the logs, and flying fish
floating through the tree tops of the swollen river.
The buzzing from the sawmills recedes behind us.
The dolphin resurfaces, leaping into the air
with a corkscrew twist of her head,
slapping her wing-like five-fingered flippers,
as if summoning me to follow her down to *Encanta,*

the enchanted underwater city of palaces, notorious
for its hidden lairs for lovers.

What is it you long for? What do you need?
Why are you craving so much illusion?

My heart drops like a rusty anchor, yanking me
down with the bluesy desire to dive off the boat
and follow her home. Strange,
these temptations to fall all right, but into reverie,
fall like stories down through the centuries
about the natives who have protected these *botos,*
legendary shape-shifters said to be half-dolphin, half-man,
and looking every creepy part of a creature on the verge
of evolving into something completely different.

Is this the winged gift? Is she a strange
angel knocking at my door?

The story goes, as all good stories should,
that the *botos* are loved because they often save
drowning villagers along the river; other stories say they're
feared because they may be the fathers of children
no one else seems to have sired.
Falling, falling, sick with confusion,
I clutch the wet gunwales of the boat,
resisting the lusty urge to ride her gleaming back,
the need for voluptuous immersion,
rapturous disappearance.

A life was calling to be lived, but how
and why I had still to learn.

Still, I hold back. I do not jump.
Though I hear her cry for me,
a cry as real as rain,
and see her pink fin
split the water,
dive, disappear.

Years later, I read the feverdreaming news
that once you've encountered a *boto*
they swim in your dreams for the rest of your life.
I only know that on the chance midnight walk
down the hill and through the rivering fog
to the banks of the bright cafe,
I have heard her cry for me,
though I dare not tell a soul.

No one,
but you.

THE TRUE MAP OF ITALY

The only place open in Naples during siesta hour
Is a dive called *Satyricon,* which should've given us a clue.
Inside are a few wayward sailors, a drunken bus driver,
And the owner, an elderly Napoliana, who cries out, *Bella, bella,*
And abruptly ushers us inside where we're accosted
By two ruby-lipsticked, black net-stockinged bar girls.
You buy us drinks, Yankee boys, mine says to me,
Which seems harmless enough to a twenty-one-year-old
Hayseed fresh out of college, an offer I can't possibly refuse.
Where you from, Joe? she asks, sounding well-rehearsed,
But before I can utter the utterly irrelevant word *Detroit*
She hoists herself onto our table, pulls up her flouncy red skirt,
Extends one long, luscious Rockette leg, purring *Here we are,*
Wrapping my hand around hers like an Old World cicerone,
Showing me how to caress the heel of her black boot.
Right around boot of Italia.
Sure, got it, I butt in. *You mean,*
where Horace was born, Apulia?
She ignores my cheap knowledge of local history,
Tonight you stay with me, here, in Napoli,
Leads my hand on a walking tour
Over the throbbing hills of Naples,
Where, it suddenly occurs to me,
Rich villas of the Romans were built
Before the volcanic eruptions at nearby Pompeii.
But you want to know where I come from?
She asks me with remarkable hospitality,
Let me show you — here, here, here,
Up in north in east corner of Italia,

Where it's very warm, very welcoming.
Very dolce, dolce, dolce.
I can tell it's true by the way
She guides my trembling hand on a silky tour
Of Italy's undulating coastline,
Then inland to the hidden
Charms of her loveliest harbor
The thrumming mysteries
Of her vanishing point.
Bella, bella, she moans,
Welcome home, my boy.
But it costs you, she groans,
With sultry *sprezzatura,*
Just 150,000 *lira,*
bella.

A FARRAGO OF FUNGOES

Fungo, n. origin unknown, ca. 1867.

No one knows who first mastered the art,
nor where the word comes from,
though it must have been, well,
great *fun* [to] *go* and hit one,
much less pronounce one,
which means gripping the first syllable
like you grip the bat — exuberantly — then
letting go of the second syllable like you
let go of the ball when you toss it
in the air — lightly —
for that whip-quick swing
that *whacks* the long, loping fly ball deep
into what Shoeless Joe Jackson called
"the thrill of the grass,"
the gorgeous, green outfield
where stout-hearted rookies chase 'em down,
whirl and throw low ropes back to the catcher
who practices his sweeping tags of invisible runners
trying to come home, then tosses the old horsehide
back to you, the grizzled hitting coach who's been hired
for your uncanny ability to hit a ball three hundred feet
"on a dime," in that poetic parabola of flight that so delighted
Robert Frost he told George Plimpton he only had one
unfulfilled wish, to watch a ballplayer hit a fungo
so high it would never come down, a heroic deed
that would give him time to contemplate
forever the beauty of a bright white ball
against a heart-stopping blue sky,

which would inspire him to write a poem
that would also never come back down
to earth, would soar and keep soaring
in the souls of readers throughout
the games that defy time,
like baseball, like
poetry.

VI

Ain't no cure for the blues.
The blues ain't never gonna die.
                —— *John Lee Hooker*

THE IMAGINARY MUSEUM

Since the reign of Augustus,
Who collected mammoth bones
In his villa on Capri, labeling them
The bones of Homer's heroes,
People have flocked to museums
To view artifacts of history,
And to cathedrals to experience
The relics of religion.

But now, as Andre Malraux points out,
photography allows us for the first time to see
the entire legacy of world art:
"The art world hitherto known to mankind
was exclusive, like religions; our art world
is an Olympus where all the gods,
all the civilizations, address themselves
to all men who understand the language of art."

Art is the "anti-fatum," in the minister's immortal phrase,
an engine of images "which deny our nothingness."
The museum without walls exists in your mind.
Its exhibitions change frequently.
Its hours are flexible.
Admission is free.
It costs nothing but
your imagination, nothing
but your soul.

DIG IT: THE RISE AND FALL
OF THE DAYS OF FUTURE PAST
a found poem

The Archaeologist

Three Valuable Prizes

To encourage the readers of *The Archaeologist* to compete
in building up our subscription list, we offer the following inducements:
For the largest number of new subscribers sent to us by March 1st, 1895:

$15.00 Cash,

and the following relics of rare form, perfection and beauty:

One good sandstone pipe. One butterfly ceremonial.
One stone Tablet. One slate ornament. One slate pendant.
Copper and shell Beads. Two grooved axes. Five celts.
Two hammers. Two pestles. Twenty good spear heads.
One Hundred arrow heads, all kinds and well sorted.
Five drills. Five scrapers. Samples of pottery.
Hematite cone and celt.

from the library at the Florida Museum of Natural History, January, 1895 issue of The
Archaeologist: An Illustrated Monthly Magazine, devoted to archaeology, ethnol-
ogy, history, etc. $1 yearly, single copies .15 cents

SANTORINI BLUE

When seen from an approaching ship
the blue-eyed domes of Santorini blend
in uncannily well with the deep azure sky.
If island folk are asked by guide book writers
why they paint the domes of their white-washed houses
with heart-stopping blue paint, they're told it's to keep them cool.
If asked by pilgrims, they'll reveal how they believe the domes
thwart the evil spirits that torment the island.
If asked by lovers after a few glasses of ouzo,
they will quote Sappho, Cavafy, and Kazantzakis
to help describe the blue fire ignited in the hearts
of those who gaze over the caldera
nine hundred feet below that
glitters with the scattered light
of crushed sapphires.
Above this ancient glory,
you set down the menu
at our cliffside cafe
and kiss me as if
for the first time,
sending a lava flow
of molten desire
down the sheer
slope of my
soul.

VINCENT'S SEARCH

> I am seeking for blue all the time.
> —— *Vincent Van Gogh*

"At last I have a landscape with olives and a new study of a starry night,"
he wrote to his brother in early May 1889 from deep within
the fingernail-scratched walls and iron-barred windows
of the insane asylum at Saint Paul-de-Mausole,

Then the grisly sliced ear episode, the agonizing night of drinking
from poisonous paint tubes, the gunshot to the empty stomach.
Theo tucked away the last of Vincent's eight hundred letters,
bundled together the final paintings, and stared at his brother's
tortuously swirling mustard-colored clouds,
ferociously drawn charcoal trees,
and weeping onion suns until
his eyes hurt like bee stings.

Theo tried to follow the twists and turns of that labyrinthine mind
that believed *painting harnesses infinity,* tried one last
time to understand the wild depths of the hypnotically
swirling colors his brother believed would save his soul
and somehow scratch his existential *hankering after the eternal,*
tried to revere the sacramental presence in everything he saw
he swore would vindicate him, tried to stomach the irony
of his brother's belief that painting was an art of survival,
a practice that "made the darkness visible and tangible."
Why wasn't that enough, Vincent? thought Theo,
as generous as ever, *Why did nothing make you content?*

If anyone knew better, it was Theo,
who knew his broken soul of a brother never
searched for more than *frankly green, frankly blue* landscapes,
only longed to paint an olive orchard so vivid others
would want to harvest it, a starry night sky so alive anyone
who gazed at it would long to lay themselves down
and sleep the sleep of the ages below it.

On the long train ride back to Paris
Theo clutched his brother's last, unfinished letter,
remembered Vincent's words about the stellar forces behind *Starry Night,*
"The sight of the stars always make me dream . . .
just as we take the train to Tarascaun or to go to Rouen,
we take death to go to the stars."

And it takes life
to return
to earth.

THE GENIUS

> The blues is truth, the truth is blues . . .
> —— *Ray Charles*

He's three years old, poor and scrawny, but still sees well
enough to spend afternoons fishing in fresh southern rivers,
then shamble down to the smoky pool hall to learn piano
from a boogie-woogie player. By the time he's seven,
his eyesight's fading, he can't see the keys anymore,
but he's already dug down into the soul of the Delta,
warmed his heart by the devil's fire, forged his crossroad blues,
donned his trademark dark shades, learned
the virtues of pure heart singing by fusing
the ache of field hollers with the rapture
of revival gospel and the rhythm
of soul-scorching blues.
Can I get a witness? for Brother Ray,
shouting, "See the mystery; ain't you glad?"
His great sculptured head swaying back and forth,
shoulders squared up over the grand piano,
his genius emerging out of a wound so deep
his eyes couldn't weep, so his voice growled
with the telltale primal *aarrgghh* one moment,
and a silvery crying time come-on the next,
C'mon, baby, love your daddy all night long,
A soul molded by heartbreak,
colored by barrelhouse blues.
Lord, have mercy.

FIGURING IT ALL OUT

One night during *les annees folles*,
The crazy years of surrealistic experiments
In art, politics, revolutions, literature,
And *cri de coeur* for the ineffable,
There was a meeting with the remarkable
Friends of the Russian mystic Gurdjieff
In one of the renowned salons of Paris,
A gathering which ratcheted
Over the gears of night and on into
The pewter gray hours of dawn

When a presumptuously tired acolyte
Yawned, stretched, and tried to leave.

Gurdjieff raised his hand,
and said imperiously,

You can't leave.
We haven't figured out yet
If God exists.

Expat mystics in the Latin Quarter
Believe their ghosts are still there,
Each one arguing for a better theory,
Which matters more, critics say,
Than if any of this ever
Happened.

MOHAWKS

Why do they do it,
Those Mohawk ironworkers,
Those highflying *karistakeronon*,
How do they do it, those daring young men
On the flying trapeze of twirling beams
They're paid to steady, fit, and fasten?
What compels them to walk an iron path one foot wide,
Ninety stories above the mercilessly hard concrete streets
Of Manhattan, Boston, or Toronto,
As cool and collected as young boys whistling
As they logroll their way across a wildly flowing river?
"For *that*, for the *story*," the former skywalking steelworker
Told me the other day as we strolled along the Embarcadero
Looking at all the new construction, me feeling battered
By the salty winds off the bay, him looking as steady
As the iron girders he'd spent years bolting into place.
His face is unclouded by fear when he says,
"Why do you think they call 'em *stories*?
We hear 'em and send down the moccasin telegraph,
Stories that prove we're strong, stories that prove we're courageous,
That we walk with the gods steadying our shoulders."
I nodded, as if I understood his spiritual warrior rap,
and was trying to raise an intelligent question about balance
or wind shear factors and fear of heights, when he added,
"Oh, and for the bread," he said.
"It pays good, man, real good."

THE FABLED LIBRARY

> In the populous land of Egypt they breed a race
> of bookish scribblers who spend their whole lives
> pecking away in the cage of the Muses.
> —— *Timon, first-century*

The night I learned the librarian at the new high-tech library
in San Francisco dumped a hundred and fifty thousand
old books into a landfill site along the bay, I thought
I heard the *merciless sound of the gods grinding*
this world to dust, while mourning all the lost knowledge,
that had been preserved by our scribacious ancestors.
That's why I riffled the pages of memory
to recall the fabled Library of Alexandria,
housed in the first real museum,
the home of the muses, those daughters of memory and meaning.
Founded in 300 BC, its core collection was the personal
library of Aristotle and Ptolemy's "book tribute,"
a papyrus scroll copy of every book seized from
every ship that arrived in Alexandria.
By the time of the biblioclasm,
the great fire in the seventh century,
the emperor's dream of a "house of wisdom,"
containing "all the books of all the peoples,"
had swelled the fabled collection
to seven hundred thousand scrolls.

But that's not what I really want to tell you.

I want to tell you about a time when books
were exalted and words were thought to be full of magic power,
which is why the librarian inscribed these words
in stone above the entrance:

The Place of the Cure of the Soul,

a reminder to all who entered
that the human spirit can be nourished
from the reading of great books,
renewed by the contemplation
of mythic images, stunned
by the staying power of stories,
which may be why Durrell later called Alexandria
"the winepress of love."

But the library vanished anyway.
No one can agree on when or why.
Some blame Caesar for ransacking the city.
Others claim that an angry mob flayed
Hypatia, the legendary last librarian,
and torched it all in a delirious bonfire
that burned for months, moving
the chronicler Epiphanius to write that where
there was once an oasis of books
"there is now a desert."

If, as the ancients said, a room without books
is like a body without a soul,
then what is a city without books?
A city without a soul?
If, as the African proverb says,
when an elder dies it is like a library burning,
when a library dies is it like our elders burning?

The possibility pounces on us
in the darkness.

The Bengali poet Rabindranath Tagore wrote,
 "The worm thinks it strange and foolish
that man does not eat his books."

Oh, but he does,
he does.

THE NEW PERGAMUM

Twenty-four centuries after the last manuscripts
Were pilfered from the ancient library of Pergamum,
Scientists are using digital cameras and infrared filters
To recover long-buried words underneath
The decorative scrolls of a medieval prayer book,
Where the parchment had been scraped away.
They have been bombarding the pages with ultraviolet light,
Causing it to "fluoresce in spots where the vanished
Tenth century ink had altered its chemistry."
Underneath the surface of the palimpsest
They've discovered "On Floating Bodies,"
A long-lost manuscript by Archimedes.
How little we know about where we came from.
How little we know about where we're going.
How much we recover by reassembling old books,
Restoring old stones, reviving stories, compressing
The wisdom of any age the way the ancient Greeks
Copied miniature *Iliad*s and *Odyssey*s to fit
"in a nutshell," which could be carried with them into battle,
And carried with them into their dreams when they
Slept with them underneath their pillows.
I have known these old books
since before I was born.

HARMONY

In 1936, when Helen Keller visited Martha Graham's dance studio
The famed choreographer wanted the young prodigy to feel

the genius of her craft in her fingertip's, which compelled her
to summon one of her male dancers, and placed Keller's hands

on his stomach muscles as he leapt in the air,
and as he held first position,

the girl felt his muscles bursting with energy, blood, oxygen,
and desire, desire, desire

and Graham studied the metamorphosis of the girl's face
as it changed from curiosity to joy,

and marveled at the bounding spirit of the body:
"How like thought. How like the mind it is."

SLEEPING BEAUTIES

The old map makers had to work with a half-complete picture
of reality, faced with the terrific challenge of how to describe
the unseen, the invisible, the unimaginable.
Their known world was like a beggar's tatterdemalion coat,
riddled with holes, empty pockets, and full of hope,
pleading to be covered, forgiven.
For the vast mystery of *terra incognita*,
unexplored lands, shores and seas,
the negative space of atlases
riddled with sea monsters, cherubs,
and intrepid explorers,
maps designed
to hold up the cosmos,
the yawning gaps of geography
the size of vast continents
[the scope of the unknown you to me]
the early cartographers
called "sleeping beauties,"
as if unmapped territory
is not a horror to be silenced,
but a dream to be awakened,
not an enemy to be vanquished,
but a discovery to be embraced.
Then why this recurring failure of ours to imagine
anything kinder, more benevolent, life-affirming?
Why do we fear what we arouse in each other?
All these unknown territory inside us,
All this unseen worlds between us to be
Circumnavigated with the ardor of explorers?

Why can't the emptiness be a wonder to evoke,
A beauty to awake, a peace to share
In the bramble-entwined castle
We have both fallen asleep in?
If there are no rules for exploration
Between lovers anymore,
It's time we measure for ourselves
The real path along the rugged coastline,
The true journey across deep harbors,
The hardest exploration into most mysterious coves
No one else can see but us.

"Here be dragons," the map makers warned
of the unknown world more mysterious
than outer space, vaster than the wildest
imaginations.

The monsters others imagined
May only be beauties waiting
To be loved.

San Luniere, France
1987

RELICS

Above the pine-scented
Mountain town of Chiang Mai, a soft mist
Hovers like the Buddha's own breath,
Which may be more than a chance description.
According to the founding story,
A tooth from Gautama's own mouth
Was carried to this sanctuary by a mighty white elephant
Who trumpeted three times upon arrival,
Tumbled to the ground, and died.
The mythic moment is commemorated
By the holy temple of Dai Suthep,
Which houses the sacred relic inside
A bell-shaped, gold-leafed *stupa*
Whose light is so brilliant in the noonday sun
I flinch, avert my eyes, unable to look any further,
An act that might appear to strangers
To be one of fear, obeisance, or reverence,
Depending on their sympathies.

I'm forced to find shade,
And to reconsider the host of strange rituals
Surrounding holy objects around the world,
Like splinters of the true cross or the milk of the madonna,
And as I do, I notice hummingbird-like tourists
Whirring in and out of the temple courtyard,
Contorting themselves to snap clever shots
Of the voluptuous *dakinis* sculptures,
The naked winged goddesses that seem to float

Around the temple, then walk away shaking
Their heads with condescension, mumbling
About the primitive beliefs of local heathens.

Undaunted, a saunter of pilgrims draped in saffron robes
Calmly circumambulate the temple, dropping shiny *baht* coins
Into dimpled tin cans, tossing yarrow sticks on the ground
So they might read divine patterns of their lives,
Then circling the shrine seven times,
Graceful as migrating geese
Following the magnetic pull
Of the earth as they glide
Homeward.

Chang Mai, Thailand
1983

THE SAMURAI POET

> All know the way; few actually walk it.
> —— *Bodhidharma*

Away from the press of crowds in Tokyo,
I saunter along a wisteria-lined stone path that winds
around the Meiji Shrine in Kyoto, and past an empty teahouse
to a small dock made of nara wood and deep devotion.

At the pond's edge a black-bereted Japanese man adjusts his
rimless glasses, hunches over the wooden railing, and rolls a pen
between his fingers. White butterflies play on his dark black hair
as he contemplates the mirror-like stillness of the water.

Suddenly, he nods decisively and rasps *"Hai!"*
like a warrior accepting a challenge. Unfurling a short scroll
of paper, he dips the beak of his pen into the nectared moment,
tasting the sweet swarm of spring colors and tea garden smells,
savoring the hovering of hummingbirds, the shimmering
of orange carp swirling by like royal ribbons, the
floating worlds of royal blue lotuses.

With bold strokes, he traces the shape of light.
His ink flows across the river of paper
like night sliding over day,
his eyes follow with a fierce
tenderness that startles me.
I'm moved beyond admiration,
to a glorious state of restlessness,
my writing hand twitching with sympathetic desire
to move pen over paper, my heart surging with desire

to feel the fire of the warrior poet's focus,
the heat of his radiating joy, even
as he steps away from the dock.

The poet rolls his shoulders, flexes his fingers,
arches his back, bows to the pond,
satisfied with having met the challenge
of tracking the path of the floating moment,
and as furtively as a lotus folding its leaves
for the night, he slips away.

On the wooden planks
where he had been standing
there is a dusky blue light,
like the afterglow left
by a conflagration of fireflies
who spent the last night
of their short-fused lives
flaring forth light
in a world of
darkness.

got to get that message home

THE GATEWAY OF THE GODS

> Once in ancient days
> I with god
> had a talk.
>
> —— *Shuntaro Taunikoa*

The colossal red gateway looms down the dewy path,
throwing long shadows across giant *hinoki* trees
shrouded in mist, their dragon wing limbs
reaching into the god-high sky.
Passing under the ornately carved arch
and past the stone lanterns,
my footsteps on the pebbled path
echo across the ancient garden.
I fall in with a shuffle of monks,
who listen keenly to the
flapping of prayer flags
in the nearby forest,
and the booming of gongs
from the Shinto temple.
Three ladies in Kyoto blue kimonos
glide into the teahouse with porcelain cups
of frothy green nirvana.

At the temple, I slip on a pair of wooden sandals
and slide open the *shoji* doors of translucent rice-paper,
through which I can see the grainy silhouette of a monk
polishing the wooden floor with a silk scarf
wrapped around his feet.
The room is redolent with incense,
animated with vivid paintings of leaping tigers

who are there, my guide tells me,
to prepare the pilgrim for any ordeal
that might await him on his journey.
"To appreciate the wisdom of your illusions,"
the monk admonishes me,
"You must follow shadows.
The way to enter Japan is to listen
as if every moment in our temples
is a test of your belief
in the spirit of the land."

Going to the temple, the roshi said, you walk the path.
Entering the temple, you leave the path.
But all along the path is the temple.

On the paths of rock gardens,
the monk confides to me,
we're asked to watch rocks grow.
If we can't, at least notice the life pulsing inside
the humbler objects of life, such as piles of fallen leaves,
fern-laced stones, the widening ripples of raked pebbles
around the central stone of the garden,
which he believes was dropped from heaven by the gods
so we might see how their blessings spread
out across the world.

At dusk, we part and I'm left alone to walk
along a serpentining path of stepping-stones,
freshly raked sand, and water
secretly sprinkled on the stones,

Coldplay
you don't have
to be alone

all designed to seize the wandering attention
of meditators, like the sudden whap
across the face of a tough monk.

The path out of the garden
shimmers with the smoke of burning leaves,
as if the day itself were burning down to the quick.

Night comes on quickly,
cool and wet with dew
that splits stones,
the monks teach,
so they, too, might
grow.

A monk knows
he is a monk
when he can
hear them
cry.

AS ABOVE, SO BELOW

> Under every deep a lower deep opens.
> —— *Ralph Waldo Emerson*

Ingloriously scuttled Gold Rush wrecks
rediscovered below the streets of San Francisco.
Long-lost amphitheaters revealed underneath the towers of London.
Long-buried brothels revisited beneath the rubble of Pompeii.
The foundations of the old French fort rediscovered along the Detroit river.
One hundred and twelve epigrams written by the Greek poet Posidippus
Deciphered on a mummy's papyrus wrappings, found in a Macedonian cave.
Stone age villages found by sponge divers in Naples Bay.

Meandering miles of the infamous Cu-Chi Tunnelplex
Reopened for tourists who want to worm below Saigon.
Thirty-nine hundred-year-old stick-figure inscriptions,
perhaps the very origins of the alphabet, discovered
on the walls of a remote cave deep in the Egyptian desert.

In a sleepy backwater village along the loamy Nile
an antiquities guard shuffling behind his lumbering donkey
in the ruins of the pharoah's palace stumbles
into a hole that leads directly to an undiscovered tomb
filled with gold-covered mummies.
A suicide truck bomb explodes in Sri Lanka,
blowing the roof off a temple housing a tooth of the Buddha,
which is called a blessing in disguise because it exposes
ancient wall paintings of an unknown ceremonial pageant.
A frozen mammoth is found buried in a block of permafrost in Siberia,
cut out of the ice with hacksaws and flown by helicopter
to a giant refrigerator in Khatanga, where it is slowly thawed out
in the hopes of isolating its DNA and reviving the species.

[handwritten annotation: The Coldplay The Hardest Part I can feel it go down]

Something that defies ordinary language
makes the soles of our feet prickle
with anticipation of what is always there,
but waiting to be finally seen,
making the back of our necks burn
with the desire to follow our hunches
in search of vanished creatures,
scuttled ships, hidden treasures,
if we turn and look back at the tree-root
we just tripped over,
trust that *frisson* that snakes down our back,
trust our strange desire to restore things to life,
trust our obsession with salvaging knowledge
and gleaning wisdom where ever we can find it.

Still, the world looks up for salvation,
reaching beyond its grasp, because
that's what heaven's for.
Living in the moment is marvelous,
the ancient philosophers tell us,
but never enough.
God help us for missing
the treasure down below.

THE COUNTRY OF BLUE

There is no blue on the walls of the Lascaux caves.
No blue in the skies of the Old Testament.
None in the eyes, veins, skies or seas of Homer.
There is *vin bleu,* but no blue tulips.
There is Bronze Age sword blue, Egyptian tomb painting blue,
and the blue ink of drowning books staining
the white-capped water of the Tigris river.
Many cultures never even conjured up a word
for nature's rarest color, that flash of peacock feather
of pigment that finally lit up the colorless sky,
as if the gods had gone back to the design
board to reanimate the world
with the divinely blue breath of life.

The sudden appearance of blue was no mere fluke.
It was a colorful passport allowing us to travel as if in a new country,
a new world where blue whales leave glinting fin-prints,
where bluebirds fly over the white cliffs of Dover,
blue morphos flit across the cloud forests of Guatemala,
and blue-footed boobies flop around the rocks of the Galapagos.
It revealed a world of blue ruin after years of drinking gin,
the *blue volts* of the poet's depression,
the flickering blue neon and soul-tumbling blues
after your woman done left you, then the starburst
motel sign outside the depression blue room
where you made love when she done come back home.
A world as blue as the seat of a Dutchman's pants,
as blue as a hitchhiker's thumb in Alaska,
as blue as the kohl-colored eyelids
of an Egyptian belly dancer along the Nile,

as iridescently breathtakingly blue
as the thin line of the earth's atmosphere
astronauts have seen from the moon.

A world of blue delphiniums, lapis lazuli stained glass,
crushed sapphire blue light, blue-streaked glaciers,
flow blue pottery, woad blue, gobelin blue,
Alexandrian copper blue, Delft pottery blue,
Memphis blue-eyed soul, Stilton blue cheese,
college stag party blue movies, blue balls, and blue screens,
Morocco's blue-handed vendors, India's blue-faced gods,
Navajo blue-furred coyotes, Viking tunic blue,

A world of Vermeer's blue-veined maids, Cezanne's blue mountains,
Bonnard's blue cornflowers, Matisse's ecstatic blue nudes,
Picasso's Blue Period, Rimbaud's blue summer evenings,
Hubble's blue-shift stars, Leadbelly's blue-bending notes,
Bunyan's blue ox, Marc's blue horses, Chagall's blue lovers,
Elvis's "Blue Suede Shoes," and miles of Miles
Davis' *Kind of Blue.*

A world where once in a while
I must remind you that if I say
I saw an aura of blue light
around your beautifully rounded belly
in those tremulous days before our
son was born it's because I saw it,
yes, I saw a light coming from within you,
and, yes, once in a blue moon
I can see it
around him
now.

It is when we near the end of a book that we enjoy it.
Guests whom we anxiously expect often fail to come.
So the world runs always contrary to our wishes.
How rarely in a hundred years do we open our hearts!

—— *Chen Shidao* [1052-1102]

EXHIBITION NOTES

SPHINX.
Inspired by an *Archaeology* magazine photograph of a skindiver swimming in the waters off Alexandria, Egypt, where the stones of the Pharos Lighthouse were recently discovered.

A PHRASE ABANDONED BY NERUDA.
The phrase from Pablo Neruda is found in his 1974 autobiography, *Memoirs*.

FOOTPRINTS.
The quotation in italics is directly from Daniel Defoe's *Robinson Crusoe*, published in London, 1719.

YOKO'S YES.
Inspired by a late-night interview with Yoko Ono, on the Travis Smiley show, February, 2004. The italicized lines are from John Lennon's oft-quoted remarks about the night he met Yoko.

PITCH DARK.
This shadowball like poem is based on a story I heard from my Uncle Cy McCann's friend, Hall of Famer Kiki Cuyler at Tiger Stadium, circa 1968.

THE HOUSE OF MEMORY.
The Titan goddess Mnemosyne was mother of the nine muses: Calliope, Clio, Erato, Euterpe, Melpomene, Polyhymnia, Terpsichore, Thallia, and Urania. The italicized quote is from the *Dialexeis*, which dates to about 400 B.C.E., and may refer to the mnemonics or science of memory by the sophist Hippias of Elis.

MEMORICIDE.
This poem was first written the night of the bombing of the Saravejo Library, as others have been moved to immortalize the tragic night. See the Serb poet Goran Simic's poem, "Sarajevo," especially the lines "Set free from the stacks / characters wandered the streets / Mingling with passers-by and souls of dead soldiers."

THE STILLNESS OF THE WORLD BEFORE GREECE.
After "The Stillness of the World Before Bach" by the Norwegian poet Lars Gustaffson.

PART II EPIGRAPH:
From Vladimir Nabakov's *Laughter in the Dark,* cited in Alexander Theroux's *Primary Colors,* a polychromatic work to which I am much indebted.

THE MEANING OF HAPPINESS.
After "Loneliness" by Irish poet and playwright Brendan Behan.

PIMP PAINTER
The ballplayer is Tug McGraw, legendary pitcher for the Miracle [New York] Mets who won the World Series in 1969.

THE WAY OF THE WORLD.
Inspired by Holmes Welchs' retelling of the tale of Lao Tzu, in his 1957 book, *Taoism,* which I read in a Taoist temple, in Manila, in 1981.

THE MOUNTAIN MAN.
The tale of the mountain man was revealed to me by the venerable soundman Al Weston, whose father is the contractor mentioned in the prose poem.

POSTCARDS FROM MENORCA.
Written in Mahon, Menorca, August, 1992.

ARS LONGA, VITA BREVIS
The cosmologist refered to here is Brian Swimme, the brilliant scientist from Pleasant Hill, California, author of *The Heart of the Cosmos* and coauthor, with Thomas Berry, of *The Universe Story.*

THE OLDEST WORDS:
Cornwall, England, Summer, 1980. Compare the legend of Ultima Thule, The Ends of the Earth, believed to be Tin Island, now known as England, where tin, amber, and gold were seized from the talons of griffins.

BLUISH

For the quote on this page, I am indebted to Roberta Reeder's 1990 biography *Anna Akhmatova: Poet and Legend,* a book I carried with me all around St. Petersburg.

DIG IT

Discovered in *Archaeology,* Sept./Oct. 2002.

THE NEW PERGAMUM

It is fascinating to note that the word *parchment* has its roots in Pergamum, the library that stored the most parchment scrolls since Alexandria.

THE FABLED LIBRARY.

Believe or not, Mr. Ripley, "wordpeckers" is a bonafide word.

THE COUNTRY OF BLUE:

The title is inspired by poet R. H. Blackmur's essay.

ACKNOWLEDGEMENTS

Many thanks to those who have read some or all of these poems, prose poems, and parables over the last twenty-five years and graced me their comments, advice, and suggestions. First and foremost is Antler, who has patiently read and generously commented upon many of these poems since we first traded limericks on the painter's scaffolding of the Western Addition, in San Francisco, back in the early 1980s. His generous spirit is matched only by his poetic genius. Thanks also to Jeff Poniewaz, Gerry Nicosia, Tess Gallagher, Jane Hirshfield, Richard Beban, Keith Thompson, Valerie Andrews, John Borton, Sid Cullipher, R. B. Morris, James Van Harper, Michael Guillen, Margaret Wright, Haydn Reiss, Gregg Chadwick, Willis Barnstone, Beth Martin, and my late friend, Trish O'Rielly.

I also want to spin a kaleidoscope of thanks towards my copyeditor Anne Hayes, who used her brilliant red pencil to keep me from turning livid blue while proofing these pages. Many thanks to the master bookmaker, Richard Seibert, for his friendship, careful craftsmanship, and his wise reminder of the old Greek saying ποιῆσαι βίβλια πόλλά οὐκ ἐστιν περάσμος, — there's no end to the making of books. And since it's closing time I would like to lift a cup of espresso in thanks to the *baristas* at Caffe Trieste in North Beach, San Francisco, who helped keep me awake these past eleven years, long enough to finish this book.

But my bluesiest thanks go out to my partner and muse, Jo Beaton, and our son, Jackie Blue, both of whom read or heard many of these poems and gave me the blue thumbs up or red thumbs down.

Phil Cousineau
North Beach, USA
May 1993 — July 2004

ABOUT THE AUTHOR

Phil Cousineau is a writer, filmmaker, photographer, worldwide lecturer and adventure travel guide. Cousineau is the author of 17 books, including the recent *The Olympic Odyssey: Rekindling the Spirit of the Ancient Games*, which has been selected by the United States Olympic Committee as a gift book for American athletes and coaches at the 2004 Summer Games in Athens. He is also the author of the best-selling *Once and Future Myths*, *The Art of Pilgrimage*, and *The Book of Roads*, as well as editor of the best-selling *The Way Things Are: Conversations with Huston Smith on the Spiritual Life*. His first poetry book, *Deadlines: A Rhapsody on a Theme of Famous Last Words*, won the 1991 Fallot Literary Award.

Among his fifteen film credits are *Ecological Design: Inventing the Future; Wayfinders: A Pacific Odyssey; The Peyote Road; Forever Activists: Stories from the Abraham Lincoln Brigade* [1991 Academy Award nominated]; and a recent collaboration with Huston Smith: *A Seat at the Table: Struggling for American Indian Religious Freedom*. He is a Fellow of the Joseph Campbell Foundation and a member of the Author's Guild.

COLOPHON

The Blue Museum was designed and typeset by Richard Seibert in Berkeley California. The text typeface is *Historical Fell*, issued by the Hoefler Typefoundry in 1994; it is a digital version of *Great Primer* cut by Peter Walpergen for John Fell, the Bishop of Oxford, in 1693. *Delphian*, designed by R. Hunter Middleton in 1928, is used for display.

The Blue Museum was printed and bound by DeHart's Media Services in Santa Clara in an edition of 1000.

Front cover design by Richard Seibert

Thank you.

MORE PRAISE FOR "THE BLUE MUSEUM"

Phil Cousineau has long been a powerful presence in the Bay Area literary scene ...
The Blue Museum comprising poems from his entire life's work, is a book readers
will be unlikely to forget. [It] contains the whole story of one man's life, the way
poets seldom do it any more — the way Wordsworth or Whitman did it, say, or
William Carlos Williams, or even, more recently Charles Olson ... At times his
epiphanies are dazzling...

— Gerry Nicosia, *San Francisco Chronicle Book Review*

The Blue Museum is a splendid book. I enjoyed every page of it. I'm thrilled for
world culture.

— Alexander Eliot, former art critic, TIME magazine, author, *Sight and Insight*

What a wonderful source of inspiration for the imagination and creative muses!

— Angeles Arrien, author of *The Nine Muses*

This poet's achievement is a deeply intimate soul-making that refuses to neither
desert a dark bloom in the depths nor ignore its deep sweetness...a storying similar
to the composition of Homeric poetry... a poetic par excellence..."

— Stephanie Pope, Mythopoetics.com

In reading Cousineau's poetry I can imagine distant strains of Miles Davis' "King
of Blue." [He] is not a jazz musician, yet he thinks and writes as one... he riffs
through words and phrases with his horn-of-choice, the pen. With each succeeding
poem, it is a delight to see how he approaches the color blue ... Had I another hand,
I would rate this book 'three thumbs up.'"

— Stuart Balcomb, The ScreamOnLine

The Blue Museum, Phil Cousineau's long-awaited collection of poems, lands him
in the company of American greats Galway Kinnell, Mary Oliver and Robert Bly.
Wayfarer Cousineau crafts powerful images of journeys from ancient Irish pubs to
Sonoma's fertile wine country.

— Keith Thompson, author of *To Be a Man*